THE
TABLE TALK
OF
W. H. AUDEN

THE
TABLE TALK
OF
W. H. AUDEN

ALAN ANSEN

Edited by Nicholas Jenkins
with an Introduction by Richard Howard

faber and faber
LONDON · BOSTON

First published in the USA by
Sea Cliff Press (limited edition) in 1989
Published by the Ontario Review Press
in association with Persea Books in 1990
First published in Great Britain in 1991
by Faber and Faber Limited
3 Queen Square London WCIN 3AU

Printed in England by Clays Ltd, St Ives plc

© Alan Ansen, 1990
Introduction © Richard Howard, 1990
Editorial notes © Nicholas Jenkins, 1990

Alan Ansen is hereby identified as author of this work in accordance with Section
77 of the Copyright, Designs and Patents Act 1988

Wood engravings by Dean Bornstein

A CIP record of this book
is available from the British Library
ISBN 0–571–16567–2

·--+--·

The publisher and editor
wish to acknowledge the Henry W.
and Albert A. Berg Collection of the
New York Public Library (Astor, Lenox,
and Tilden Foundations), where the manuscript of this book is preserved, and to thank
the curator, Dr. Lola L. Szladits. They are also
grateful for the help and encouragement of
Leslie Estevao, John Hollander, Benjamin
Ivry, Patrick Lawlor, J. D. McClatchy,
Edward Mendelson, James Merrill
and Robert Rushmore.

·--+--·

AA

Contents

Foreword

On October 2, 1946, when W. H. Auden started a series of lectures on Shakespeare at the New School in New York, a young scholar and poet called Alan Ansen was in the audience. Ansen, who had graduated summa cum laude from Harvard in 1942, was already steeped in Auden's work, and, as he says in the Afterword to this book, he "seized on the opportunity to hear the poet in person." Amongst the drafts, quotations, telephone numbers and journal entries in his notebooks, Ansen started to keep a record of Auden's critical observations. Within a few weeks, Auden and Ansen struck up what was to be an enduring friendship, and Ansen also began to write out snatches of Auden's more digressive post-lecture chat. Before long, he was a fully initiated member of the "circle," and from that point, when he took on the role of secretary and amanuensis, his notes of Auden's private talk grew more obsessive and elaborate as his record of the lectures became scanter. Between November, 1946 and April, 1948—when this private feat of impersonation was terminated by Auden's departure for a holiday in Europe—Ansen filled four bound composition books and eighty closely-typed loose sheets as he dashed down what he remembered Auden saying. *The Table Talk of W. H. Auden* has been quarried from those pages.

These talks occurred just as the portable tape-recorder was replacing the Conversation with the Interview. What Alan Ansen created, though, will not really fit into either category, because Auden was never aware of any obligation to moderate or refine his comments. When, for instance, he protested on March 16, 1948 that "Americans have no conception of privacy," he can have had no idea, Ansen tells me, that his words would ever be fixed in print. Nor, for many years, did his interlocutor. However, since 1976 when Ansen gave many of his literary manuscripts to the New York Public Library's Berg Collection, snippets from these notebooks have appeared in a number of works on Auden. In light of this, a separate published version seemed appropriate.

This book does not pretend to be a polished literary work, nor is it a verbatim record of what Auden said as he put on his spectacles in Goody's Bar, or even a full transcription of Ansen's notebooks. (The jottings on Shakespeare, for example, are unfortunately just too elliptical and fragmentary for publication.) In preparing the manuscript, editorial intervention has been necessary in order to bring the text to the point of basic readability. As Ansen poured out his memories of an encounter, a particular topic often came back to him haphazardly, crowded out for a moment by unrelated phrases and ideas which themselves needed to be caught before they vanished. As a result, I have been obliged to yoke together some remarks on similar themes. Material given under one date in the notebooks has in a few instances been moved into a more resonant context here. (There are indications that Ansen himself may have written out several days in one sitting and accidentally misdated some comments.) Minor asides and eruptions have been dropped so as to spare the reader almost incessant changes of tack (although, be warned, what remains is still a bumpy ride), and some minor stage business such as Auden choosing a watch strap has also been omitted. One or two of Ansen's unsuccessful attempts at English idioms had to be straightened out, and I have here and there tightened a phrase. Otherwise, opinions and facts have not been altered.

My tampering has been strictly limited, though, by the desire to preserve as much as possible of the texture of Ansen's writing in the notebooks. His rapidly sketched version of Auden's talk is an interesting technical achievement in itself, and it conveys a dynamic sense of Auden's voice. However, in spite of the raw flavor, the reader should remember that the words printed here are reported speech, not quotation. What was actually said has been diluted, shaken up in Ansen's mind, and then given the occasional stir by the editor.   *N. J.*

Introduction:
The Police Undone in One Voice

It comes as a surprise, even as a paradox, that the poet who in his own lifetime instructed friends to destroy whatever letters he had written them should have inspired two volumes of remembered conversation, markedly discrepant but both purporting to record his very self and voice. Howard Griffin, who died in 1975, fashioned his *Conversations with Auden* into equal-opportunity dialogues (published in several periodicals between 1949 and 1953, but covering or uncovering largely the same period from which Ansen's *Table Talk* so variously derives). Griffin was concerned to establish his own worth as a talker, a thinker, a writer, and he took pains to work up his eight pieces into a semblance of literary form (the genre of "table talk" or *ana* is variously susceptible to such determinations: Luther, Johnson, Coleridge, Byron, Whitman, Berenson, Gide, Valéry, and Cocteau immediately flock to mind as enabling examples of this imposed form), so that when Auden read one of them, in May, 1949, he wrote from Ischia: "Many thanks . . . for the dialogue. I don't remember saying a word which you attribute to me, but I seem to agree with what you say, so it must be all right." Ansen's text is a very different matter. An accomplished and singular poet, he has chosen to edit himself out of the picture more sedulously than even the promptings of a pursued conversation would imply; frequently the sudden switches and reversals within a paragraph suggest that the interlocutor (anything but Blake's "idiot questioner") has suppressed his transitions, the modulations of argument—rather in the manner of Frank O'Hara's "Franz Kline Talking," an *Evergreen Review* piece which had begun as an interview but from which O'Hara excised himself altogether, so that the discourse has the air of a sort of *found essay*, an impromptu lecture. Still, it is astonishing that in talk taken down—with whatever degree of fidelity—at the same period, there should be so little overlap. Except for two remarks about children (that they cannot help but find all descriptions of the sexual act to be pornography, and that they should nowadays be trained either as physicists or ballet dancers—"then they'll escape"), there is an entirely different cast to Auden's discourse in the Griffin dialogues and in the Ansen table talk. The titles suggest why: there is no question, in Ansen's record, of argument, of correction, in short, of dialectics. It is not truth which is being pursued here, but characteristic locution, immediate utterance. What we have before us is a unique instance of *verbal presence*—the cranky, perverse, even on occasion wicked movement of the poet's voice and mind, with all its impulsive and wayward horrifics, as well as (nearly) all its creative illumination of *res publica* and *ars poetica* in about equal measure.

.   .   .   .

   "Goethe always Schillered when he wrote to Schiller, didn't he?" Edith Wharton said to Berenson in 1917. "That's the reason why, generally, transcribed talk is so much more satisfactory than letters. People talk for themselves, apparently, and write more for their correspondents." From my own experience of his (still extant) letters, I cannot imagine Auden writing more for his correspondent than for himself, but let us allow Mrs. Wharton's assertion to stand. It is certainly true that there is no concession made in this little book—even to Ansen—which might delete or dilute the *pour soi* of Auden's table talk; indeed the table at which such talk is spoken seems scarcely to be a convivial one, but something of a solitary's board. Hence the unmitigated gall of the decrees and fiats, the preposterous verdicts about women as actors, about homosexual fidelity, about. . . . But of course it is of no use whatever to point out the hundreds of instances where Auden is "wrong." The point is that here are instances where he is, supremely, Auden—most happily when he sustains his remarks with some fund of experience, but always valuably, indeed invaluably, in sounding that note of sharply perceived relations—in art, politics, religion, sexuality—which is so easily recognized as his own. Hence my title, for if it was remarked, and remarkable, of T. S. Eliot that "he do the police in different voices," it is comparably to be observed that Auden's critical intent—"criticism should be a casual conversation"—is precisely to undo that ventriloquial policing; to outtalk the police. Irresponsibility, even, in such conversation becomes a kind of liberal testament. Indeed Auden is hard on the great singular American critics—*i.e.*, Burke and Blackmur—who developed a style enabling them to gain access to their insights beyond "casual conversation." He was even harder, I remember—though in these monologues the subject had not been sounded—on the moralism of Winters and Leavis. And we can suppose what he would have made of the current modes of post-structural critical discourse. It is apparent that the unbuttoned talk so readily presented here is the magma out of which the poet created—or it may be the dross left behind from—*Nones* and *The Dyer's Hand*, and that the informality ("the only character I can still identify myself with in opera is King Mark") of both occasion and utterance is apparent only. More than any poet who has been known to speak at all, Auden says what he means, when he does not mean to say his poems. There are poets whose table talk we may regret not having (or not yet having: Merrill, Jarrell, Brecht)—but there are also poets who are incapable of talking at table (Stevens and Perse come to mind, though the former wrote his own *adagia* and the latter was reported to be a terror at Washington dinners). Nonetheless, the genre represented here is one which has its strict exemplars, and we can be grateful to Ansen for understanding the form and fulfilling its terms so brilliantly.

Indeed I have been hasty in remarking that Ansen rules himself out of the reckoning so entirely. There are moments when the compositional hand may be discerned, as when at the end of of the session of March 19, 1947, after WHA had said: "You seem to forget that I don't approve of Pound's politics at all. I think he's crazy. And he likes that horrible old bore Confucius. . . ." To which AJA returns: "I guess you wouldn't care to see Canto LXXX then?" And then Auden ends by saying, "Oh yes, I should like to." A bit of shrewd characterization—Auden's interest in poetry overwhelming fixed principles of morality and taste—is achieved merely by this sign-off exchange, whereupon in the next session we proceed to the question of German guilt and political responsibility in general ("Oh yes, I certainly do vote. I think everybody ought to vote in a democracy. They really ought to do what they do in Australia— fine people who don't vote"). But of course one's curiosity is roused, is exacerbated by the appearance of these discourses so long after the fact of their utterance; apparently Ansen was a prodigy of notational skill who far outreaches Eckermann (remember Cocteau's crack about Goethe throwing spitballs at us over Eckermann's head?) in exactitude of rhythm and interval. As for Auden himself, one is delighted all over again by his large devotion to a classical order of letters (the unexpected emphasis on Dante), and terrified by his insights which may well be blind spots: "Wilde, after all, is important not as a writer—he couldn't write at all— but as a behaver." "The Kinsey report is very bad . . . he paid too little attention to anal activities. A useful piece of pornography though." The preoccupation with music, with opera and its repertoire (this is the period when WHA is undertaking *The Rake's Progress*), is often prophetic in its predilections: would Auden have guessed that this very season he might have seen *Giulio Cesare, Les Troyens* and *Lulu* at the Met? He refers to such works as adored but recondite experiences of the record-collector: "Why don't they do. . . ." And as always the reading-lists are incentives.

·   ·   ·   ·

A word about what might be called the right use of these conversations. I believe this little book and its more innocuous predecessor—like the other examples of the genre, from Eckermann (Goethe) to Horace Traubel (Whitman) to Mme. van Rysselberghe (Gide)—should display a label like the one which appears on certain pharmaceutical products: NOT TO BE TAKEN INTERNALLY. Wystan Auden may have had, as Josef Brodsky often tells us, the most acute mind of the twentieth century, but its splendors were reserved for his poetry and for his literary criticism (the best of Auden's prose is in the tradition we trace from Dryden to Johnson to Coleridge to Arnold to Eliot: the poet's line, neither academic nor journalistic, but exact and eminently useful—one of the great successes of discursive literature). The table talk, like any gossip, is the agreeable (and egregious) extension of what WHA used to call "human unsuccess"; we are happy to have it, but we must not hold it against the poems. Theirs is the light by which we read— by which we read, even, this table talk, which the poems cast in fascinating shade.

R. H.

I NVITED by WHA *for a cup of coffee at his apartment, 4E, 7 Cornelia Street. Decor of apartment: anteroom with sink and stove and a large wooden drawing table on the other side of the room. In main room two deep, comfortable chairs in brown velvet, separated by a table. A stern cot with a blue blanket. A row of books in a long bookcase. A set of the* OED. *My offer to dry the coffee dishes was rejected—no hurry about it.*

WHA

I've moved from 57th Street. Too expensive. A student of mine at Bennington with whom the superintendent seems enamored of got me this apartment. I'm going to be the Charles Eliot Norton Professor at Harvard next year—$12,000 a year. Now I'm going to show you pictures of my first gr-e-a-t loves.

AJA

People from *The Waves?*

Exaggerating, WHA *pulled out books, opened them and showed eager me pictures of pumping engines. He'd brought the books with their pictures back from Birmingham on his last visit to England. He affirmed his affection for, as well as his understanding of, the pumping engines. He showed me some illustrations from* Icelandic Legends. *Grinning, he showed me photos of landscapes and pictures of himself as a little boy and books on visits to mines by frightened early Victorians.*

AJA

I should think you might almost be ready to issue a volume of collected prose.

[1]

WHA

I don't think so. Criticism should be a casual conversation. Hemingway is terribly limited. His technique is good for short stories, for people who meet once in a bar very late at night, but do not enter into relations. But not for the novel. Why doesn't he do stories about rich people? Yes, I think we're due for a revival of a Gothic, baroque prose style. Of course, it'll go too far. But we've had enough of Hemingway. James's syntax is really quite simple.

AJA

What do you think of James Farrell?

WHA

Very dull. After all, Studs Lonigan should have been drowned at birth. It's very unfortunate, but when a character has absolutely no free will it becomes very boring. Farrell doesn't *see*, and so all the splendid material about Chicago goes to waste. Studs Lonigan never does anything interesting, anything to help himself. Of course, Farrell wrote that way partly in reaction to the *Saturday Evening Post* stories where the characters are almost infinitely free. Naturally, you can't use that type of character even if he exists. Too much freedom won't do either.

AJA

I tended to be rather surprised at your adapting *The Duchess of Malfi*. Were there any inset lyrics?

WHA

No, nothing like that. I only did it for the money. I didn't direct, just adapted. They had a good director who was gentlemanly, but firm. But he left. The actors today really need the whip hand. They're so lazy. They haven't got the sense of pride in their profession that the less socially elevated musical comedy and music hall people or acrobats have. The theater has never been any good since the actors became gentlemen.

AJA

Since Henry Irving.

WHA

Since Charles II. . . . . Empson pointed out that English theater has declined since the abolition of subplots. I wonder why they went. Of course, the introduction of realistic stage design made sudden shifts of plot more difficult. Empson's a very good critic. He really feels deeply about poetry. Not like some of those boring articles in the *Southern Review*.

Jay Laughlin had a good story about Elisabeth Bergner. She was in bed, in a bed-jacket, reading Barrie's *The Boy David*. Turning up her eyes, clasping the book to her chest, she said, "Barrie didn't write it, God did." Bergner is quite easy to get along with by herself, but with others it's not so good. She does things like rattling the teacups. Canada Lee—he played Bosola—is simply impossible. He doesn't understand what's going on. I was giving John Carradine some lines to say, and he told me, "I'll say them, but I won't live them." I haven't had much trouble with the Isherwood plays. Dame May Whitty was always extremely good to work with.

A Christmas Oratorio was written before *The Sea and the Mirror*. It's the only direct treatment of sacred subjects I shall ever attempt. My mother had just died, and I wanted to write something for her. I hesitated before deciding in which order the two things should go.

You know it's impossible to represent Christ in art. We've got used to the Old Masters because they're formal, but in their day those pictures must have seemed outrageous. You can see Him at birth, or after He's dead. Perhaps after the Resurrection, but show Him healing the sick or blessing people because they have faith, and the interest shifts to those people. You can use a model, but when you're through, all you've got is a model. The two natures of Christ correspond to Essence and Existence.

AJA

How about Bach? The scene in the *St. Matthew Passion* in which Christ inaugurates the Eucharist is certainly convincing.

WHA

Yes, but there it's a direct quotation from the Gospels, a matter of feeling brought about through the music.

AJA

If we take Christ as myth it can be done. Look at Michelangelo's *Risen Christ*.

WHA

Yes, if you take Him as a solar incarnation. The myth goes back farther than Michelangelo—to Andrea del Sarto. Of course, Michelangelo began as a Platonist, but at the close of his career. . . . It's impossible to represent a saint. It becomes boring. Perhaps because he is, like the *Saturday Evening Post* people, in the position of having almost infinitely free will. That's why Uncle Tom is uninteresting.

AJA

Surely that's not fair! What about Tolstoy?

WHA

He never actually lets his characters become saints, does he? They're always on the road. In Dostoyevsky they're usually tainted with lunacy if they're saintly. That's what saves Don Quixote who, of course, is a saint. St. Paul talks like a saint, but one can't recognize a saint except intuitively.

AJA

I wonder if you're fond of works of casuistry?

WHA

I think Cardinal Newman is quite good: *The Grammar of Assent, The Idea of a University* and some of the *Sermons*.

AJA

The Catholics tend to overemphasize him at the expense of some of their other great writers.

WHA

Some Catholics don't think so well of him at all. Cardinal Manning didn't even think he was a Catholic. He was against the doctrines of Infallibility and the Immaculate Conception.

AJA

That really destroyed the chances of Reunion.

WHA

The chances of Reunion collapsed after the Council of Ratisbon in 1541. Some of the more liberal Cardinals had hit on formulæ of reconciliation, but the Pope squelched them. And that was the end of Conciliar authority. It's a shame. The Protestants have become tied to nationality, the opposite of a universal church. At first the Catholics were accused of being too worldly. Well, that's all right, that's a temptation to everybody. But later they were disliked because they were Italian and Irish.

AJA

Some of their best people are English and German.

WHA

Yes, but they're very hard on them. You know, they hate Maritain but keep him because he's so useful.

AJA

Did you enjoy Brecht's lyrics from Denmark: *"Schlage keinen Nagel in die Wand"*?

WHA

No.

AJA

Perhaps you enjoyed the *Dreigroschenoper*?

WHA

Yes, I saw it in Berlin.

AJA

A good deal of demonstration, I suppose?

WHA

No, the Nazis weren't much in evidence then. Political street fighting didn't begin until the elections of 1932 when the Nazis got so many seats. In 1930 they seemed forlorn and were begging shabbily on the streets for funds.

AJA

Are you read much in Germany?

WHA

It's impossible to get books into the country. Several people I correspond with in the Russian zone have got in the black books of the authorities. Not because they corresponded with me, but that shows what happens to people with regular æsthetic interests.

AJA

I didn't know that you had taught at Bennington.

WHA

Yes, for one term, while someone else was away on a Guggenheim fellowship. Bennington is positively a brothel, you know. Around eleven o'clock one night I heard a knock on my door. A girl came in and simply refused to leave—insisted on staying the night. Oh, they're nice girls, all right. But they talk. The next morning they rush to the telephone and tell everyone all about their night. It used to be that people were more reluctant to tell than to do. Now it's the other way round.

At this point I rose to take my leave.

A FTER the lecture I lingered for a moment and caught up with WHA, *showing him my day's acquisition, Kierkegaard's* For Self-Examination and Judge for Yourselves!

AJA

Do you have this?

WHA

Yes, I think I have them all now. I may not have some of the edifying discourses published by obscure houses, but I don't think I want them very badly. Why don't you come have a drink?

AJA

Grand. Do you really think Shakespeare would have approved of your interpretation of his work?

WHA

I don't care whether he would or not. It's in the text, and that's what counts. As a matter of fact, I think that Shakespeare's young man was only a would-be Prince Hal—a failure really. Shakespeare wrote the plays with a double idea: to show the young man how horrible that kind of character could be, and to show him what a real success is. And it is Falstaff who is really remembered.

AJA

Have you a particular bar in mind?

WHA

No, we're going up to my place.

AJA

Actually, one feels jumpy about being intrusive.

WHA

Oh, in that case I shouldn't have asked you. Don't

[7]

worry, I'll kick you out early. I'm working just now on the Betjeman anthology. I've just finished my book.

AJA

The Age of Anxiety?

WHA

Yes, it's frightfully long. I don't know how it is, being
so near it.

AJA

I was extremely depressed by one of your reviews I
was just reading this afternoon—your review of Miss Phare's book
on Gerard Manley Hopkins. You were terribly kind and said it
wasn't her fault but the university examination system's.

WHA

Oh, one doesn't know what to say when reviewing a
book one doesn't like. Really, it's a mistake to write long reviews
of books that aren't any good. Just note that they've been received
and perhaps a short summary. I think that's where the *Partisan
Review* goes wrong: spending too much time with people who
don't matter. Of course, if one had a chance to do something like
The Robe, where one could do a very elaborate and detailed anal-
ysis of an important, bad work, that would be different. Wilson's
demolition of MacLeish shows far too much study of him, far too
much concern.

Entering the apartment, I saw that WHA *had a new green
velvet couch in his room.*

AJA

Have you read *Religion und Kunst?*

WHA

I find Wagner's prose inexpressibly tedious. I read the
piece about the Jews in music and something about the origins
of language. How were you able to read through his work? The
piece on language in *Oper und Drama* was full of *Urelemente—*
perfectly ghastly. One doesn't feel much humility. Even Parsifal
triumphs. And in a perfectly worldly way becomes King, wins

the Grail. What will you have to drink, sherry or red wine? I
think red wine is better for this time of night.

*He filled two tumblers a quarter-way full. Throughout
the evening, he filled his own twice to my once.*

It's astonishing how little American fiction makes of
money. If one were a novelist, one could describe a passionate
love affair and with it all the details of the menus and how much
everything cost. Even F. Scott Fitzgerald, though he gives you the
atmosphere, doesn't present the facts. How much, for instance,
could be done with the Crash, its effects on people's lives.

AJA

With that point of view, I'm surprised that you and
Isherwood on your Chinese trip found Trollope so unpleasant.

WHA

Oh well, you see, Trollope wasn't *specific* enough.
There was a certain whitewashing. Now Balzac, *there*'s a great
writer about money. It's amazing how shy Americans are about
talking about money matters. They will tell you the most intimate
details about their sex lives, but shut up like a clam when you ask
them what salary they're making. They talk about English reti-
cence, but the first question Englishmen ask each other is "What's
your salary?" Last year for the first time I went to a Miss Stern to
look after my income tax. When she'd finished I was amazed. I
thought I'd go to jail. She deducted everything, even photographs.
People in America care so much about money. You really must
treat it like fairy gold.

You know, it was very good for me to have had to go to
work for a living after leaving college. If I'd been a rentier—there's
a difference between rents from lands and income from stocks or
city real estate—I'd have done nothing but debauch continuously.
The rentier doesn't do well in America. He takes to drink. He
must move to Europe. The pleasure of flouting the neighbors

leads to drinking and so forth to impress them. A tremendous number of people in America work very hard at something that bores them. Even a rich man thinks he has to go down to the office every day. Not because he likes it but because he can't think of anything else to do. But now, I must say, I really wish somebody would die and leave me a nice bit of money. Now I really think I could do better on an income.

AJA
I tend to be something of a parasite myself.

WHA
I see no reason why one shouldn't work for the Luce papers or *Town and Country*. As long as they leave your stuff unchanged. Oh, they can change a word here and there for the sake of perspicuity. What difference does it make? Of course, once they ask you to change a line of thought, that's prostitution. You have to withdraw at once. I have no patience with people who tell me I must give an article to them cheaper for the sake of a cause. Always sell in the highest market. Sometimes you may get five hundred dollars for a piece that you consider very minor indeed. And again, you may get only twenty-five dollars for something to which you've devoted a great deal of energy. Fairy gold, fairy gold.

I was down in Washington last week with the National Guild of Episcopal Scholars. I'm a member. I had a paper to read. We went to a terrific number of services during the day, four or five. The complines were particularly terrifying. You know, they were composed when the barbarians were at the gates of Rome.

AJA
I shouldn't think that you'd find them at all unsuitable.

WHA
Oh no, though that particular danger doesn't seem especially imminent in Washington now. The world certainly makes us appreciate these things more cogently. But it's amazing how malicious the tongues of those Episcopal Scholars can be. Why is it, do you suppose?

AJA
Perhaps it goes along with the sin of gluttony traditionally ascribed to the clergy. There's no outlet for other energies.

WHA
Yes, I suspect so. One man in particular seemed to take anyone who disagreed with him as his personal enemy. Just like a Common Room. It really does remind one of Oxford dons.

Oh, I had occasion once to visit the Pentagon and, really, that's straight out of Kafka. When I was just going through a gate to get out, a guard stopped me and said, "Hey, where do you think you're going?" I answered, "I want to get out." And then he said, "You're out already."

AJA
Was this before you went to Germany?

WHA
No, afterwards. I was really quite frightened and kept having these rather Kafkaesque dreams.

During the war, the FBI came round to investigate me. Some of the people thought I was a spy. The FBI man said, "You're a Scandinavian, aren't you?" They obviously thought I'd come off a submarine. He was really very nice. He said, "I noticed you going into a restaurant with a book, and my heart sank. I thought you'd be in there for hours." I said, "Why didn't you come in?" "I didn't want to embarrass you," which was really rather nice.

When I was delivering my Phi Beta Kappa poem in Cambridge, I met Conant for about five minutes. "This is the real enemy," I thought to myself. And I'm sure he had the same impression about me. He is the real Prince Hal and gives the notion of sheer naked power. I took the line of chiming in with him, of being terribly cynical about politics. Of course, I didn't feel that way at all, and I'm sure I didn't take him in for a second.

You know, I should like to ask him whether he was the one that made the final decision to drop the atomic bomb. The scientists got a pledge from Roosevelt that the bomb would not be used until an announcement had been made. But then, of course,

Roosevelt died, and after that. . . . One shrewdly suspects that Conant gave the deciding word.

AJA

I should hate to think that. I'm not sure I'll ever see Conant again, but if I did I should like to be able to speak to him.

WHA

Oh, I don't feel that way at all. If I *knew* he was responsible, I'd go right up to him and say, "Why, you old fox."

I related the story of a friend's criminal experiences.

WHA

You shouldn't be truculent with the police. They expect people to be angry and afraid. You must be naive and wide-eyed, look at them as a friend. But when it comes to specific details, be right there with the facts. When I was getting my citizenship papers, I was asked whether I was a Communist. Then they asked me what newspaper I read. I could answer the *Times*. The man—he was an Irish Catholic—asked me whether I read the *Daily Worker*. I didn't think that was an altogether fair question. I didn't read it habituallly, but I've occasionally looked through it. I answered, "Yes," though. He asked me whether I'd read Karl Marx. I answered, "Yes." He asked me if I thought there'd be any changes in the world in the next fifteen years. I was quite intrigued with that one. Finally, he asked me if I were a Fabian socialist and if my wife was charging me with infidelity.

AJA

It would be rather interesting to see what someone who was *au courant* and appreciative, yet politically hostile, would do in that position.

WHA

Oh, I'd simply refer him to the relevant passages. But this man wasn't a fool. Look at the question about Fabian socialism. The questions are simply in case someone makes an inquiry in Congress. They have to show they've been diligent. I spoke to the man afterward. He's a graduate of Notre Dame.

You know, it's frightening how easy it is to commit murder in America. Just a drink too much. I can see myself doing it. In England, one feels all the social restraints holding one back. But here, anything can happen.

AJA

I hope that you will confine yourself to pricking yourself with a penknife every day like Goethe.

— WHA

(*Smiling.*) There are many things in Goethe I dislike very much, but I recognize myself in him sometimes.

I saw a man killed recently on 4th Avenue and 20th Street by a policeman as I was returning from Lexington Avenue. He'd been in a holdup and had got in a bus and had drawn a gun on the driver. The lights, unfortunately for him, had changed, and the policeman shot him through the window. Nothing happened to the passengers. But you can imagine how they must have felt. It's really unsafe, especially now, to be on the streets after one A.M., with more than a dollar in your pocket.

About six months ago, I was a witness in an extortion case. A friend had two people literally draw knives on him. He had no money and telegraphed me for some. Of course, I sent it via telegraph. It had to be collected in person, and when my friend got there he vaulted over the barrier and yelled, "Call the cops!" One should always call the police.

AJA

What is the connection between "Victor" and the end of "The Temptation of St. Joseph"?

WHA

Victor was really somebody by that name. Joseph is me. Victor was at a school where I was: he used to send anonymous letters. He'd told us he'd already done it, evidently hoping no one would suspect him.

AJA

Or perhaps to get sympathy in advance. Wasn't Mrs. Victor very angry with you?

WHA

There wasn't any Mrs. Victor. I defend Edith Gee against all comers. I've been told I was too cruel, but it's actually true. I've seen it. But the best one I ever did was never published. It deals with a fashionable woman. The objects on her dressing table started talking to her. She committed suicide. I showed it to a lady who promptly tore it up. Not for any personal allusion, but because she felt it was an outrage on the sex. I had other copies, but I don't know what happened to them. I may do some more.

January 8, 1947

*W*ALKING *home with* WHA *after the lecture.*

WHA

Brünnhilde is not a young woman. She is as old as God and much heavier. Perhaps my dislike of Brahms is extra-æsthetic. But whenever I hear a peculiarly obnoxious combination of sounds, I spot it as Brahms and I'm right every time. I feel the same way about Shelley. He's the only English poet I really dislike. His rhythms can be very nice, but his diction is impossible. Very bad. Browning's way is not mine, but I can admire him. The lyrics are atrocious, but the longer poems are not. "Bishop Blougram's Apology" is a tremendous achievement. Browning is the first poet of the lower middle classes. *The Ring and the Book* isn't really a myth. Dostoyevsky could have done it better. You read Browning and keep admiring the prosody—the brilliance—but all the same, somehow it won't do.

Blake's longer poems won't do either, with all that fantastic background. I don't dislike Wordsworth at all. He is especially good in his longer pieces. *The Prelude* is a marvelous work. I like the same country as Wordsworth but not the same places. My landscapes aren't really the same as Wordsworth's. Mine, and that's a point I haven't written about yet, come from books first.

Firbank is very good. I'm fond of Disraeli, who gives something of the same effect. His characters are so good. I don't see how you can parody him. Firbank is really very tough underneath. His father wasn't Director of the London Northwestern Railway for nothing. He doesn't claim to be the whole world—just a small window on reality.

The real test of liking English poetry is Pope. His ideas

aren't much, but the language is wonderful—"*Chicane* in furs." *The Rape of the Lock* is the most perfect poem in English.

Who could translate Catullus? I think Cummings would be very good at that.

AJA

Do you think Rilke would be any good?

WHA

He is too *schöngeistig*. He simply could not bring himself to translate "*Pædicabo ego vos et irrumabo.*"

AJA

But he would do "*Odi et amo*" quite well.

WHA

Yes. Pound, if he weren't dotty, could do Martial. But his Catullus would have too much hair on its chest—a slight weakness of the Propertius.

Verdi and Mozart are the top composers, Alpha plus. Bach, Beethoven and Haydn are Alphas. The supreme Verdi work is the *Requiem*. I don't feel Mozart keeps up quite so well. They object to the violence in the *Requiem*, but a requiem is for the living. Haydn is really a better symphonist than Mozart. The top Mozart is in the operas and concerti. I have *Figaro*, *Don Giovanni*, *Zauberflöte*, and *Così*. *Così* is really marvelous. It looks a little like Firbank but is ultimately major.

I have just been discovering Verdi over the past five years. Aside from the last three operas, I am fondest of *A Masked Ball*. They've restored it to the setting in Sweden. *La Traviata* is a great work, conceived beyond the soundness of smiling socialism. The second act of *Parsifal* is really wonderful, except for the Flower Maidens' scene. Non-Wagnerians prefer it, but I don't like the plot of *Die Meistersinger*—partly the exaltation of art, partly other things. The only ones I like all through are *Die Walküre*, *Götterdämmerung* and *Tristan*. In the *Ring* my order is *Walküre*, *Götterdämmerung* . . . that wonderful oath on the spear. The duet between Brünnhilde and Waltraute. There's one that, when you consider the billowy soprano, is really quite funny: *"Das ist kein Mann."* One thing I don't like about *Parsifal* is the emphasis on virginity. Of course, celibacy may be desirable, but that isn't saying that if you aren't celibate you are excluded. The whole idea of the Grail, the sacred object, is essentially heretical. Everyone should have an opportunity. All that Good Friday performance of *Parsifal* is terrible. I don't mind the church coming into art. The church bells ring like mad in Italian opera. But in *Parsifal*, it's taken so seriously. That business of no applause is bad. The way Wagner thought he was writing something simple and popular when he started *Tristan* is amazing.

You know, *Tristan* should really be done by two "lizzies." They eat each other up, try to replace the world. Isolde is the English Mistress, Tristan the Hockey Mistress.

Don Giovanni is a certain type of male homosexual. Neither extreme, Tristan or Don Giovanni, is compatible with heterosexual love.

Kierkegaard ought really to have heard *Tristan*. Oh, he might not have liked it, but he would have been fascinated by it. He would have written something brilliant about it.

Some of the material in the B-minor Mass is really out of this world, but there are long dull passages. But think of the *"Qui Tollis."* I really only like the *St. Matthew Passion* as a whole. I was brought up on Bach and heard him all the time when young. But I really realized the *Chaconne* was boring. Bach one likes to play oneself rather than hear. The *48 Preludes and Fugues*, for instance. The *"Kyrie"* seems marvelous for the first two sides, and then you realize he's going on with the thing to the bitter end.

The *Missa Solemnis* is Beethoven's greatest work, I think. I don't mind the part that follows the *"Resurrexit."* Wagner once said, late in his career, "I adore Rossini, but don't tell the Wagnerians."

AJA

I began with *Carmen* and then went on to the Germans.

But *Carmen* is a very great work. I'm personally fond of Liszt, though I don't insist on him for other people. The opening of the *Totentanz* is so good. (*Sang it.*) But why does MGM hire people to write music for them? Liszt has done it so well already. I think Hofmannsthal is the one librettist you can read apart from the music. The Marschallin's speech. (*He quoted it.*) Da Ponte's libretti are quite good. The *Italian Symphony* is really very pretentious music.

It's amazing how unhappy good American critics are when they read a good writer who is also a bad man. Like Curzio Malaparte's *Kaputt*. If he weren't a fascist, how could he get access to all that material?

Samuel Johnson is a person not much appreciated in the United States. And the people who do like him are either like Yvor Winters, or nasty types of Anglophiles who think they have to be rude and are usually Republicans. But Johnson was a great melancholic romantic and he wrote some exceedingly acute things. In Ben Jonson I'm especially fond of *The Alchemist* and *Bartholomew Fair*. *Volpone* is really too unpleasant. My favorites now are the masques.

GOING home with WHA *after class.*

WHA

Randall Jarrell is really just trying to flout Papa. And the simple mistakes of fact! I'm glad you caught him so nicely on the "moment of choosing." Of course, he is really quite a good man; that's what makes his mistakes so irritating. You spotted the point about "O Tell Me the Truth About Love." For me personally it was a very important poem. It was written in the Mediterranean on a ship in 1938 on the way to China. Christopher spotted its importance at once. It's amazing how prophetic those things can be, because it was just after that that I met the person who did, really, change things for me so completely. Just as in a poem I did in the early thirties I had not only Hitler, Mussolini and Roosevelt, but Churchill too. He was really only an unsuccessful politician at the time, but he'd just won a by-election.

I'm really a sanguine person. I've always found existence enjoyable. Even when one is hurt and has to bellow, still one is always fundamentally happy to be able to. If I had money, though, I shouldn't live in America. The climate is bad. I should like to live somewhere in Southern Europe. Formerly, I should have liked the Balkans, the Carpathians, or a castle in Transylvania. I should have liked to travel a great deal. Greece would have been too dangerous and too hot. I might have ended up in Hammerfest. Perhaps it's just as well I didn't have any money. I've taught everything: Arithmetic (I once thought of doing a series of arithmetic textbooks), Drawing, French, Latin, History. To get along, you have to flirt with the headmaster's wife, play golf with her and let her win. Then you must establish yourself as the school's one

buffoon. (No school is allowed more than one.) I'm almost sorry
to have left high school teaching, but the work is too demanding.
Twelve-year-old boys are the best people to talk to. They're so
intelligent. They get tremendously interested for about five minutes, then forget all about it.

Anyone who has a child today should train him to be
either a physicist or a ballet dancer. Then he'll escape. It's amazing
how mercenary scientists are today. They work for the other side
quite cynically. It's very dangerous to be a poet, and even a musi-
cian isn't always safe.

During the twenties they used to have resident poets at
Michigan, but Bridges spoiled that game by behaving extremely
rudely and refusing to speak to anyone. Now they make you work;
you have to give lectures and so forth.

I really retain a sneaking fondness for Bridges, you
know, though Eliot is perfectly devastating on *The Testament of
Beauty*. He lived at Boar's Hill. He never really left Oxford. But
Matthew Arnold and W. P. Ker are the only really great men who
have held the Professorship of Poetry. De Selincourt, yes, he was
a good scholar. I tend, you know, to be very much in awe of
scholars—they know so much about their field. And even when
one feels they're wrong and one's right, one doesn't have the facts
to prove it. It's a disgrace they haven't offered it to Eliot, a man
with a really international reputation, just the sort of person for
the job. And why hasn't he received the Nobel Prize? How they
could ever have given it to Pearl Buck, I don't know. Sinclair
Lewis, after all, does stand for something. It may not be your cup
of tea, but still there it is—*Babbitt*, *Dodsworth*, *Arrowsmith*. But
Pearl Buck. . . .

Eliot does realize his danger of falling into a Manichæan
condemnation of the flesh *per se*. But our poetry is the product of
our feelings. There's an awfully revealing anecdote about Eliot.
A woman who was seated next to him at table said, "Isn't the party
wonderful?" He said, "Yes, if you see the essential horror of it all."

I came to America because it's easier to make money here, to live by your wits. Bennett Cerf told me how he was entertaining a European writer at lunch at the Plaza during the twenties. Before lunch he bought some stock, and he sold it afterwards. Next day he sent the writer a check for three hundred dollars. It's so wonderfully tempting, so easy to get money without working. Take this man who started out in 1923 with only three hundred dollars and got it up as high as ten million. Of course, he lost most of it later, but he ended up with three million, and I'd be satisfied with that. There were plenty of warnings of the Crash, and some people ended up with a good deal of money. The mechanism of investment is fascinating. Balzac is so good on that. I'm a capitalist now. I have a mortgage on a house in Sea Cliff on the North Shore, so now I can drive the widow out into the snow on Christmas Eve. It takes, if you look at the successful businessmen around, a rather low order of shrewdness.

The nineteenth century, outside of Ibsen, had no drama, but how rich it was in opera. Wagner, Verdi, Donizetti. I've just bought *Don Pasquale*. How good it is, and how little one hears it. Donizetti may have written cheap shoddy works, but I don't know them. *Lucia* and *Don Pasquale* are so good.

One thinks of Shakespeare as sitting quietly in a corner and then, when he'd had quite a bit to drink, becoming screamingly funny.

I'd like to hear *Les Troyens*. I know quite a bit of earlier German opera. "*Ozean! Du Ungeheuer!*" is well done by Flagstad. I'd like to hear Hugo Wolf's opera *Der Corregidor*. Yes, "*Ganymed*" is amazing, but they got John McCormack in his later stages and he sings it so badly. I have two Wolf Society albums. Have you ever heard *Israel in Egypt?* In some ways it's even better than the *Messiah*. It has some wonderful fugal choruses. Why don't they revive Handel's operas at the Met, I wonder?

In my contract for *The Age of Anxiety*, I specified that I wanted to have control over the details of printing. Now they bow and scrape whenever I come into the office. They used to treat me like an unwelcome office boy. But I don't like all this kow-towing. The man in charge must be very annoyed over having to make a fuss over me since he must think I blame him for the things I don't like—and I do. The book is going to be very small, the poetry is set in very small type and the prose still smaller. I think it might be very attractive to print a book of poems in white type on black paper. I'm amazed no one here knows what a "gasometer" is. I wanted to use it for *The Age of Anxiety* and couldn't for that reason. I was heartbroken. I want the poem to be completely American in language.

My two ambitions are to get into a history of English prosody and into the *OED*—have them cite me for new words not yet received. It's a shame I can't write lines backward as they could in inflected Icelandic.

Christopher and I did a very early play together, but it hasn't been published. I'm not worried about his being a Hollywood writer—he's very tough. What really concerns me is his Vedanta. I've written to him about it, but that sort of thing isn't very satisfactory by letter. They're really like the Stoics and Epicureans in their detachment. It's exoticism, too: Christopher's interest is a revolt against England.

WHA

Around Lydgate's time the language started to decay. Even Chaucer had to warn about mispronouncing his writings. Why don't the Communists model themselves after Virgil? He's wonderful for the business about the historical mission of the special race. Aeneas isn't just a private person. The Russians are giving up their ideology for the Slavic race—very alarming. I've told you about those German friends. The Russians have banned Wagner, whom they ought to like so well—race hate against the other Germans. Dostoyevsky is such a great and such a naughty genius with his Pan-Slavism. That's why I like him so well: he's so naughty.

The trouble with America is that the separation between the artist and the politician is too complete as compared with England or France. I don't mean giving official posts like the one they gave to MacLeish. But they should be invited to dinner. We'd get into the White House through Margaret and her interest in opera. Truman would be a little hard to take, he's so thoroughly lower middle-class. Somebody called him "a little West of center." Jefferson, I think, must have been a great bore. One compares him with H. G. Wells in the present period, but the difference in taste is a good sign of what's happened in the course of a century. One began with a prejudice against Lincoln, of course, but the more one reads of his sayings, the more one feels he was really a great man. I like his remark to the man who said, "Let me shake the hand of the man who saved the Union." — "Sir, you may be more than half right." I like Taft because he was so fat—you know, he needed an extra-large size bathtub. Jackson really began the process of anti-intellectualism. I don't think you can say that Lincoln was a faker. Yes, Hamilton was really brilliant.

One wonders whether Roosevelt developed paralysis in order to become President. No, I didn't think *you* were sickly—nervous people seldom are. It's usually the stupid people that develop long illnesses. You need more than indolence and selfishness, you need endurance to make a good patient. Proust was as strong as a horse. He needed his illness to force him to write.

Yes, "*Cæli, Lesbia nostra, Lesbia illa*" was the one I liked so much. Nietzsche had a good aphorism: you can profit by illness—if you're strong enough. I got through all the conventional diseases at boarding school. They're more dangerous when you get older. Childhood diseases give you a chance to rest from growing. Today children are retarded far too much. I wonder what new disease is going to become especially virulent—as the common cold did after the last war. Measles has been getting increasingly serious in the past fifty years. I'm going to live to be eighty-four. Of course, I can't tell where I'm going to die. It would cause a great stir if it ever got out, but you know, when I was young I used to play piano duets from *Tristan* with my mother. My mother used to get ill every time I came home, which gives you some idea of the relations between us. I resolved very early in life, though, that I wasn't going to be a victim to that sort of thing.

Nicolson was probably too brash for Proust, and Proust probably found out that he didn't belong to any of the more exclusive English families. His wife did. Gide is really commonplace. The ideas behind *Les Faux Monnayeurs* are exciting but badly executed. The end is a masturbator's daydream—so optimistic. The *Caves du Vatican* is much earlier. This business of being absolutely honest! And when he was getting off with this Arab boy, stopping to say, "*Que le sable était beau! Que le sable était beau!*" One simply can't say that under the circumstances, it's *ausgeschlossen*.

I've been reading an exciting Old Welsh epic written about events that took place around 600. There are interesting forms in the Welsh, which is printed on one side, though I can't read Welsh. You know, primitive poetry is always obscure. You could make a great defense of hexameter poetry along those lines. People are still interested in crossword puzzles and riddles. I don't like crossword puzzles because poetry has more relevance. If you would present highbrow poetry as a superior type of riddle with a definite answer, it might catch on with a good many people. Yes, the highbrow critics would feel a little lost.

I couldn't get through *Thésée*. It was too boring. He has no *solidité*. I'm essentially anti-French. La Rochefoucauld simply says what one has always known. I don't care for him at all. The French writers I like are atypical: Pascal, Baudelaire, Rimbaud, of course. Baudelaire is so good about Frenchmen worshipping Voltaire. I don't like Montaigne at all. He was more unhappy than he pretended. In the present generation, I like only Valéry and Cocteau. Cocteau is extraordinarily clever. Valéry is very intelligent. A monster, if you like, but tremendously intelligent. It's the tremendously intelligent ones I'm interested in— Pascal and Valéry. They really go beyond the conventional Gallic intelligence.

In adapting one looks for raw observations that hadn't occurred to one before. Nietzsche really beats the French at their own game. Amiel is a bore. Who are the greatest aphorists? Pascal, Baudelaire, Nietzsche, Blake, Kafka. There are wonderful things throughout Kierkegaard, especially in the *Journals* where they occur almost continuously. You can often pick them out of Newman.

Betjeman is really the only person who really understands many of the things that are important to me. That's why he got it. (*Presumably the dedication to* The Age of Anxiety.)

The Episcopalian organists over here are 20 years behind the people in England who've rediscovered the nineteenth century English religious composers. I told one that the music he was playing reminded me of 1912. I'm afraid he was insulted, but that's really where American organ composition is—still in revolt against the nineteenth century. Mother and I used to do the Grand March from *Athalia* on the piano.

I cut out the Housman poem because I felt it gave a false impression of my attitude towards him. I do think it's a good poem. My reasons are not æsthetic. So much of Housman is based on hymn tunes. (*Sang "Stolen Waters" to hymn tune.*) Morgan Forster said in his review of *Further Poems,* "We may hope that Mr. Housman had the opportunity to taste of the 'stolen waters.' "

He started singing the appearance of Jesus before Pilate from The Passion According to St. John *with perpetual* "Und Jesus antwortete." *He quoted with satisfaction Pilate's* "Was ich geschrieben habe, das habe ich geschrieben."

Yes, it's very good. The great "*Da gedachte Petrus an die Worte Jesu, und ging hinaus und weinete bitterlich*" comes in *The Passion According to St. John,* especially the word "*weinete.*" Wagner owed more to Bach than any other composer in the interval did. The whole musical-pictorial technique links them. I was so happy to notice that the first performance of *Tristan* and the publication of *Alice* came in the very same year—1865. I saw *Romeo and Juliet* recently—some very nice music, but unfortunately Gounod's work came two years after *Tristan* and imitated it extensively.

I don't like the Catholics going back to Gregorian chant for their music. The great Catholic music is in the operatic masses of the nineteenth century. *Tristan,* of course, goes back to *Norma,* which Wagner liked very much. The Catholics aren't escaping from the æsthetic by taking up Gregorian chant even though they may think they're showing good taste. They get rather boring. I can't stand Palestrina. I agree with Nietzsche completely. He just goes on and on.

AJA

I've been listening to the Pope's address to the Catholic schoolchildren. The Irish announcer came through clearly, but the Pope's English was rather hard to follow.

WHA

I don't think it was such a wise idea for him to broadcast in English. You get the impression this is another dirty wop, an organ grinder. The Catholic chaplain at Columbia and other Catholic friends tell me that people like the Pope, that he's a good man but a little foolish. It is hard to believe. Of course, he's taken in by Spellman. I'd very much like to know the real inside story of the Vatican: it must be the most exciting place in the world, where spirit and world come closest together. That's where I'd like an official job most of all.

I'm very fond of King Christian. In Copenhagen before the war I used to see him bicycling about. But when the Germans came he went around on a white horse. There was a news report that he had a fall and was going to die, and I wrote a poem about him. But then he recovered, and I had to scrap it. The only two English kings with taste were James I and George IV. James wrote quite good poetry. The evidence for George is Brighton Pavilion. I'd like to know more about William III. George V was the first English monarch since the Stuarts to speak English without an accent. Edward VII had a terrific one. George really saved the monarchy. Edward VII's goings-on had made the bourgeoisie quite bitter. And there was a great Republican movement during Victoria's time. But George's conduct during 1914–1918 changed people's feelings. And his willingness to go along with the Liberals on the budget and create additional peers. . . . The Tories were furious with him.

It was fine the way everyone was agreed over what Edward VIII ought to have done. People have no conception of the thing here in America. I think the idea of marrying her must have been a whim of his. By that time he was completely in her power. H. G. Wells' Republicanism doesn't count. Edward VIII had such dangerous friends—as people in his position are likely to have. Shaw was just being amusing when he made the monarch active, and he's Irish anyway. I am a convinced monarchist.

There's a wonderful anecdote about George V. The Earl of B. hadn't been around the court for a while. George: "Where's B?" Courtier: "He's left England, Sir." "How's that?" "He had to leave the country, Sir." "Why?" "Homosexual, Sir." "Humph. I thought they shot themselves."

George V was dead when I got the King's Poetry Medal—he died in 1935. I've seen four monarchs. Edward VII, George V, Edward VIII, and George VI. If that horror Elizabeth marries a commoner, he'll only be prince consort.

Why doesn't the United States take over the monarchy and unite with England? England does have important assets. Naturally the longer you wait, the more they will dwindle. At least, you could use it for a summer resort instead of Maine.

What a spectacle it was when Virginia Woolf and Stella Benson decided to run off together and their husbands pursued them to the airport. Oh, they finally persuaded them to come home. But what a wonderful scene for a movie!

WHA

Are there any Catholic priests in Russia? I've been talking to my friend who works at the broadcasting station sending
to Moscow, and he's very depressed. He thinks there'll be a war in
five or ten years. He's a Russian, you know. Yes, indeed, I really am
very anti-Russian. I never was actually a Communist, though I was
more or less on the verge at one time. My trip to Spain opened my
eyes to a good deal, but it wasn't only that. Almost all the people
who returned to Russia after a period of emigration are either dead
or living under the most frightful conditions. Those horrible gold
mines! They got Mirsky during the '37 purge. Then X was actually
begging on streets, sleeping under bridges. And Y was discharged
from his official job and thrown out of his apartment, which he
could only hold as an official. These are people I've been told are
very good and I send stuff to them. It's the Russians' horrible
Romanitas.

There's a story of how the Russians point to a couple
of windows with a bee inside and say, "There's Stalin," the busy
bee. And the Ribbentrop-Molotov Pact of 1939. . . . It's true the
Russians had a good deal of reason to be offended with England
and France at that time, but to do what they did was unpardon-
able. No, the slave labor business is absolutely wrong.

You know, I can't stand the French. Baudelaire was
absolutely right when he talked about "*l'esprit de Voltaire*." I suppose Voltaire and the others performed a historically useful service,
but they're such vulgarians. More than any other country, the
French really look to Rome. No, not the Vatican, the Roman Empire. I can put up with Byzantium but not with Rome. The only
reason the Protestants and Catholics have given up the idea of

universal domination is because they've realized they can't get
away with it. The Russians believe they can, and the aftermath of
this war has helped convince them. Nicolas Nabokov says the
one hope for peace would be if Stalin died. Not that the others
are any better, but there would be such internal confusion that
they couldn't fight a foreign war. The United States would be
worse off than the Soviet Union in an atomic war. Its industries
are comparatively centralized. Of course, the first objectives won't
be industries but the enemy's atomic bombs. Espionage will multi-
ply tremendously. The war could be won in two weeks. If you got
the bombs there couldn't be much retaliation. Of course, there
are barbarians here as well as in Russia. Colonel McCormick and
the editor of *Pravda* are perfectly interchangeable.

   Hitler had to be smashed completely. That was the first
job. But then you had immediately to help the enemy with all your
strength. The English understood that. Of course, one couldn't
think so at the time, but there really is something comic about
Hitler's speeches, especially the one to the General Staff. The new
material published on his last days underground in Berlin, all that
long-range, thousand year planning, Hitler orating madly when
they were at the end of their rope. It really has its ridiculous side.

   The Allies made a great mistake in not cooperating
with the July 20th conspirators. They were the elite. They didn't
go around thinking everyone was as good as everyone else. They
knew they were superior and so had greater responsibilities. And
they acted accordingly. That's what I can't stand about the French.
During a war they lie down like a doormat, and afterwards they're
meanly vindictive. People were tremendously shocked by the
French surrender in England, even the ones who kept defending
them. Of course, I don't have any use for the type of opinion that
says the French lost because they were too sexy, or something
like that. Were you in Paris before the war? Well, it was really
horrible. They almost *wanted* the Germans to come in. The French
petit bourgeois is the most disgusting specimen of humanity you

can think of. And the way they kept using German prisoners of war as slave labor. At least in England there would have been protests over that sort of thing. They must be either a great power or a small one. They can't keep up their frivolous foreign policy if they want to be great. And if they're going to be small, I don't want to hear a peep out of them on the subject of politics, not a peep.

At least the Russians have a serious foreign policy. You may not like it, but at least it's serious. England is really the only country with a continuing serious foreign policy that realizes the central importance of balanced forces. I'm afraid the United States has a rather frivolous foreign policy. It is a great world power now, after all.

The trouble with the French is their terrible Cartesianism. To them, you agree or you don't agree. And that's perfectly logical. But it doesn't find any place for the irrational element which is always present. And so they stagger from anarchy to dictatorship and back again. The concept of His Majesty's Loyal Opposition is absolutely foreign to them. The English, without being so nationalistic, are really more of a nation. They don't talk about "*la gloire*" and "*la patrie*." The English were fortunate in having their revolution earlier, and they were wise enough to keep their nobility open to fresh talent. I find it easier to sympathize with Laval than Pétain. Laval was just a crook and made no bones about it. His conduct at the trial was marvelous. But Pétain really pretended to be good.

Napoleon was really the precursor of Hitler. The Germans, after you've said everything there is to say about the inflation, the depression and the disorder, are really culpable for having chosen Hitler. They knew what they were getting in for.

If France is going to be a small nation, it should be like Denmark. There's a wonderful country. Under the occupation the people's behavior was absolutely correct. No collaborators, or only a very few.

No, I think the Existentialists were absolutely phoney. During the nineteenth century those little groups were important, but this is just a pale imitation. They don't have much in England, but at least they keep quiet about it. I think that's far more admirable, really. In France their good people are all older or dying off. I don't much care for Eluard. Camus is better than Sartre. And the reactionaries in England aren't such diehards as they are in France. If change comes, well, they'll fight like the blazes to stop it but they'll adjust—get used to it. For the French, change means the end. They can't imagine the future, any future. And they don't have any really good humorists. There's nobody like Sydney Smith, or even Shaw, in France. No, I can't stand Anatole France. Rabelais isn't very amusing. They have nobody like Nietzsche either, who can be screamingly funny—the only German writer who is. Montaigne is really dull. And Gide. I don't like Montaigne at all. *You* see France as I see Ireland—a country of bucolic charm.

I've been increasingly interested in the Jews. Here's a book I've been reading about the Jewish mystics, the Chassidim. There's one man who was the Jewish St. Francis. These were all eighteenth century. Here's a blessing: "May you be as healthy and strong as a goy." These mystics all lived in Poland. I wonder what would happen if I converted to Judaism. Most people of that type turn to Mohammedanism—no, not Hinduism, that's something different. I wonder why there are so few converts to Judaism. I don't know about Hebrew schools, but if they are anything like the Sunday school I went to, they must be pretty awful. There's nothing religious about them, perfectly pagan. I expect if you went to a really Orthodox school it would be all right, but the Reformed are impossible.

AJA

One would like to ignore politics completely.

WHA

But they are necessary. You can't do without politicians. The newspapers can certainly be very wicked. But you can pick out decent people writing in them all the same. Yes, there are decent people making their voices heard from time to time. Mrs. Roosevelt for instance. Every position she's taken has been the right one. He certainly can't have that said for him. No one really good can get to occupy the position he did.

But still, Roosevelt was much more decent than Hitler. Or Stalin, for that matter. And after all, he could have rejected the good things he was taught at school, but he didn't. Of course, Hitler is much more interesting æsthetically, but you can't judge æsthetically. That's sheer romanticism. Have you ever read *Mein Kampf*? It's really the most honest book any politician has ever written. He did everything he said he was going to do. You'd think the Germans would have had to ban it. Hitler was so conspicuously evil. Have you read the reports of the Nuremberg trials? Well, there's one spot where Hitler is talking to the staff on August 23, 1944, late in the war, and they really sound like characters out of Dostoyevsky. The English too are succumbing more and more to *Romanitas*, but at least they still scream about it. South Africa is the worst country in the world. I simply can't stand Smuts. If he meant what he said, he should have resigned long ago.

Yes, I'm lecturing on the Quest—at Barnard, though, not at Columbia. I began with the Argonauts, then *Odyssey* (the quest for responsibility), then the *Aeneid*. I'm going to do the Grail tomorrow. Then we'll do *Don Quixote* and so on. The students, though, are a rather stupid lot.

Do you know Dorothy Sayers' book on art and the Trinity, *The Mind of the Maker*? It's awfully cunty, but very good.

The Catholics haven't really evolved a Christian æsthetic. They didn't take over Aristotle's metaphysics, so why persist in a pagan æsthetic? After all, they didn't condemn works of art as being unchristian. Even St. Thomas relies on Aristotle's æsthetic. In fact, one wonders just how Christian he was. The thing that reconciles one to him is the great vision he had in the closing days of his life when he said, about his work, "It's all straw." You remember what Kierkegaard said about Hegel: "If he'd only said after he'd written his books, 'It's all a joke,' Hegel would have been a great man."

And the unsureness of the Catholic Church in dealing with the movies is another example. They have a good answer for almost everything—contraception, for example. But their attitude towards manifestly heretical movies, which they let by, is thoroughly inconsistent.

You know, I'm beginning to feel that even Dante isn't really a Christian writer. He's really *the* greatest poet. It's amazing how much harder it gets when one has come to take things seriously. Before I became a believer it was easy to accept Dante's theology and suspend disbelief. But now I'm coming to doubt whether he really was a Christian. He doesn't realize that God suffers. Dante's Hell consists of punishments imposed from without, not of sinners who deliberately stay there, which is the Christian belief. On the other hand, I don't see how a non-Christian can make sense of *Don Quixote*. If you think the double nature of Christ is so much nonsense, there's no meaning to Don Quixote and Sancho Panza. And you begin to wonder whether you ought to write religious poetry at all. When you're writing romantic love poetry, you know it's all frivolity. But when you write religious poetry, you're not so sure, so you may begin to feel that it's really important. When you go to Mass, it makes absolutely no difference whether you're emotionally excited or not. Religious emotion, like any other kind of emotion, is irrelevant to religious duty. No, I don't think it's wrong to write religious poetry. But when you write religious poetry, the tension is so enormously increased, you keep wondering. . . . But it's time for you to be off; where's my watch? I must have left it at the New School.

March 17, 1947

Did you listen to Margaret Truman last night? I did.
She was really awful, especially in that aria from Delibes. Have
you ever heard Florence Foster Jenkins? She kept appearing on
the concert stage and had the most awful voice imaginable, so bad
that she became a smash hit. People flocked to see her and laugh.
And she never realized that people didn't think she was marvelous.
Her "Bell Song" from *Lakmé* was really something. And her
records—unbelievable. She dressed fantastically. You know, I think
she must have had masochistic leanings. Oh, on the surface she
thought she was wonderful. But underneath. . . .

Lawrence's poems on animals in *Birds, Beasts and Flow-
ers*, some of his short stories and travel books are wonderful. *Lady
Chatterley's Lover* is sheer pornography. There's only one good
test of pornography. Get twelve normal men to read the book,
and then ask them, "Did you get an erection?" If the answer is
"Yes" from a majority of the twelve, then the book is pornographic.
That's all. Don't you agree? It doesn't make any difference what
the author intended.

But Lawrence has so much dialectic behind it.

It's still pornography all the same. You have to see the
sex act comically, as a child. Just as descriptions of the beatific
vision are indecent. The sex act is at the precise other end of the
scale. And descriptions of both are really indecent. Yes, the sex
act is the other extreme—more than strangling. In the sex act the
Spirit has to hide its head, whereas in the beatific vision. . . . I can't
really read the poems of St. John of the Cross. They make me feel

[35]

embarrassed. And you will notice how much these beatific visions sound like the sex act. And the Pseudo-Dionysius just keeps telling you the beatific is not this, it's not that, until at last you blurt out, "For Heaven's sake, what is it?" If they don't know, they had much better keep quiet. The real way to talk about the beatific vision is the way Aquinas did. After having the vision he said what he did about his work, "It's all straw." You're really convinced he had a genuine vision.

Pascal just limited himself to a few scattered words. He never intended the *Memorial* for publication as he did the *Pensées*, but hung it around his neck like a scapulary. And he wrote those wonderfully malicious *Provincial Letters* afterwards. How he must have enjoyed doing them!

Dante's case was quite different. He didn't pretend to have the vision himself. He was simply a poet asking himself how would you describe Heaven.

═══════════

A̲T tea, in company.

WHA

I think that poetry is fundamentally frivolity. I do it
because I like it. The only serious thing is loving God and your
neighbor. Because you can say, "I'm not a mathematician," or "I'm
not an artist, and that's all right because I have no talent for it."
Everything that isn't required of you is fundamentally frivolous.
Now you can't say about loving your neighbor that you have no
talent for it. It's required of everyone. No, it isn't harder for one
than another. It only looks harder to the individual who is con-
fronted with his own problems and can't see someone else's. Of
course, the human race as a whole is unlovable. If it weren't, there
wouldn't be any problems. Yes, you can see that some people have
a special propensity for evil.

Someone asked him what he thought of Jeffers.

WHA

I don't express myself on people who are still living. I
only talk about people who've been dead a long time. If a surgeon
tells you he operates out of love of humanity, that's nonsense. Of
course, you hope it will do some good, but fundamentally you do
that sort of thing because you like it. No, I don't think I write in a
modern style just out of will. It depends on one's feelings in the
matter. One writes to please oneself. It's not so conscious as all
that, though of course it's not entirely unconscious. If you have
to know exactly what was on my mind when I wrote something,
you'll never be able to read it.

No, the process works this way: first I convert my feel-

[37]

ings into a variety of algebraic symbols, and the reader turns them back into subjective impressions. Any interpretation that will stand up is all right, unless you can point to the text and say, "See here, it says thus and so."

Someone asked, "Why is your work so obscure while Spender's is so clear?"

WHA

I don't talk about things like that.

A middle-aged man of Spanish or Latin-American origin started to ask about the Existentialists and Gongora.

WHA

Yes, I've read Neruda. But Gongora isn't just sound. If you're just sound, you won't seem like anything in translation into foreign prose. And Gongora is perfectly amazing in English translation. Even Poe, who is much more inclined to that sort of thing, is much more than just music.

AJA

Who would be a good example of a poet who is very good on sense, not so wonderful on sound?

WHA

(*Quickly.*) Browning. He doesn't become really good until he's read in bulk. "Bishop Blougram's Apology" is magnificent, but the magnificence is in the psychology. The shorter pieces are pretty awful. But the great ingeniousness of the work is undeniable. I think I'd better go. (*Outside, to me.*) Come along and have a drink. That was really horrible. And that question about the Existentialists. . . .

AJA

Have you ever calculated the frequency with which the question comes up?

WHA

Yes. And he obviously didn't give a damn what I

thought about the Existentialists. I don't mind that sort of question from an eighteen-year-old, because he really wants to know. But this man is too old for that. He simply wants to hear himself talk. And that gets me angry. (*Stopping at Goody's.*) What do you think of this bar? I only know the MacDougal Tavern. I haven't been inside a bar for years.

He led me to a table with red checkered cloth, put his briefcase in one corner and sat down beside it, leaving me to face him on the other side. He ordered old-fashioneds, I burgundy.

There are two things I don't like. To see women drinking hard liquor and to see them standing at bars without escorts. Women should drink port with lemon. Oh, after you've been riding or something like that, you can have something stronger. But in general, no.

AJA

I understand someone is doing a master's thesis on you.

WHA

Oh, yes. Ken Lewars, at Columbia. Ken is married. He's being psychoanalyzed now. He's rather dull.

AJA

I think that people with special knowledge, though they may be dull, can be useful.

WHA

If you want special knowledge, there's just one place to get it from. (*Presumably himself.*)

The one good thing Galsworthy did was a play in which a character ate himself to death on the stage. *Hamlet* could never be put on the stage. I've seen the Stratford performance. Not very good. I think that the business about Hamlet's making the King drink the poisoned cup should be done slowly and brutally.

AJA

Why not use the Quarto text—that way you would

have a shorter play and be more faithful to Shakespeare.

WHA

As a matter of fact, the Quarto play isn't very good, you know. If an actor wants to do it, all right, let him. Really you would need a Southern Italian, a Sicilian, to do it properly, with tremendously theatrical gesticulations. As a matter of fact, Hamlet ought not to be played by a Northern European at all. The British are too restrained. My brother-in-law Borgese would do it wonderfully.

Why don't English and American actors have the same discipline that the people at the Comédie-Française do? Not that I think that the things they do are so wonderful. Racine isn't quite so fine as people say. But they can make their voices do anything they like. The French language does lend itself to that more than the English. But still we could do more of it than we do. People are so much better educated that way in France. You can see at a glance the relation between one's concierge and Racine—you can't do that here. I like to write out long speeches in French and use outrageous but permissable words like *"se tartuffiser."*

You know, for three years, I had to eat lunch every day with a horrible jukebox blaring away. It was in a drug store at Swarthmore. There was no other place to eat. I thought I'd go out of my mind if I heard "I'm Dreaming of a White Christmas" one more time. And did you know that little ditty "There'll Be a Hot Time in the Town of Berlin"? That reached peaks of popularity in 1944, but it stopped abruptly about the time the Battle of the Bulge began. The jukebox is really an invention straight out of hell.

AJA

In some places I think there are slots where you can put in a nickel and get silence.

WHA

That's a wonderful idea. It would be well worth *fifty* cents just to get that much uninterrupted silence while you eat your lunch. I don't see why you shouldn't. It's a free country. But the height of malice is reached by the people who simply walk into a place, put a nickel in the slot, and walk out again without even staying to listen to the tune. No, you never really get used to it. I don't see why you have to have noise while you're doing things. Washing the dishes isn't particularly pleasant, but it's perfectly easy to think while you're doing that or shaving. Out at Fire Island I tend to let the saucepans get rather black at the bottom. The one thing I will not do is bury the garbage. There's a boy out there who's going to be President of the United States, and he's getting an early start by burying people's garbage. Mine gets buried every two days in the sand. It disappears in winter. (*An old man, his upper torso bent forward at right angles to his lower torso, emerged from the washroom.*) What a perfect image of contemporary civilization! Did you see him go in?

Oh, hadn't you read *Notes from Underground?* Some people think it's the best thing he's done. I'm especially fond of *The Possessed.* It's so terribly funny. All those jokes at the expense of Turgenev. And very serious at the same time. *The Idiot* I find a little severe. It's something of a discipline to read, what with Prince Myshkin.

Do you dislike D. H. Lawrence's letters as much as I do? They're almost as bad as Rilke's, which are so *schöngeistig.* And so are his girl friends I've met. So awfully *schöngeistig.* No, they're not all rich, but they're intelligent.

AJA

You know, someone was trying to sell a copy of Groddeck with your notes in it to a friend of mine.

WHA

Then whoever it was must have stolen it. I've been missing it for some time. Now, Alan, I'd appreciate it if you played detective and found out about it for me. Then I'll simply go over there and say, "Please let me have that book back. It's mine."

AJA

You'll have to write a poem for them first.

WHA

Not at all. They'll simply have to hand it back.

AJA

Have you seen the new Pound canto in the September *Poetry*? It sounds quite mellow and sane. For instance he talks about the Germans having lost the war because they didn't like mathematical music.

WHA

(*Making a little moue.*) You seem to forget that I don't approve of Pound's politics at all. I think he's crazy. And he likes that horrible old bore Confucius. The man was right who said, "Thank goodness only one country has chosen an insufferably dull person for its national hero—China."

AJA

I guess you wouldn't care to see Canto LXXX then?

WHA

Oh, yes, I should like to.

You mustn't blame the Germans for complaining. After all, most Americans would probably behave just as badly in a similar situation. Even now they bow so much to the tyranny of public opinion. No, the Americans have no right to criticize. And besides, what may seem like absolute self-pity in an Englishman or an American often isn't so in a German. It may just be their way of showing a feeling of intimacy with you. The people who weren't Nazis are really taking their revenge on the people who kept their jobs under Hitler. And the occupation authorities seem to work on the mistaken principle that those who joined the Party early were the worst, but they might have been actuated by a sincere idealism. Whereas those who joined after the Purge. . . . The authorities seem to favor liberal theologians too. You know, all the liberal theologians after '33 in Germany became German Christians.

Oh, yes. I certainly do vote. I think everybody ought to vote in a democracy. They really ought to do what they do in Australia—fine people who don't vote.

Have you seen R. G. Collingwood's *The New Leviathan?* It's printed like aphorisms, with numbers.

AJA

Like Wittgenstein!

WHA

Or Spinoza's *Ethics.* You know, that's the way criticism should be written. Oh, I have quite a lot of Variorums! I wish I had more. They give you quite a history of academic lunacies. What are the really good books of criticism, the ones that basically influenced me? There's W. P. Ker. Hardy taught me stanza forms, but Ker really made me see the perpetual availability of metrical forms, and related prosody to general culture. Eliot's *The Sacred Wood* was in a way a very important book when it came out. By 1935 the revolution in taste among people who concerned themselves with such things was complete. Still Eliot remains without doubt the greatest selector of quotations in English. He knows exactly what passages will provide the greatest stimulus for further reading. I don't see much point in doing that sort of thing for Shakespeare. But where a writer isn't so well known, then it's fun. Another book that for all its faults remains important is Richards's *Principles of Literary Criticism*. Yes, I know it can be very misleading, but it does ask the right questions even if it comes up with the wrong answers. It makes one think about what actually does happen when you read a poem, which people hadn't thought about before. And Empson's two books. The man writes with such genuine passion for the books he's discussing. With so many critics you feel they're writing so people will say they're good critics. Yes, you're right, he isn't quite sound on Milton, but you can understand the temptation to get him into the book.

Another wonderfully passionate work is Nietzsche's *The Case of Wagner*. I never really cared for Wagner till I read it. It's superficially anti-Wagner, but you sense how much he must have cared. And the way he hits off the Wagnerians—professors, failures—who soak themselves in him and pay no attention to what is meant. Do you know Lawrence's *Studies in Classic American Literature*? Let me show you. He led me to read Cooper, but I couldn't take very much of him. One of the *Leatherstocking Tales*, I think. I've read two books of Mark Twain: *Huckleberry Finn* and *The Mysterious Stranger*—the one about the Devil. And I don't want to read any more. I may have dipped into *Pudd'nhead Wilson*. *A Connecticut Yankee in King Arthur's Court* is really the most vulgar work in English. *Huckleberry Finn* is all right to read once, I suppose. At least he's better than Corneille. The man I really hate is O. Henry—those horrible trick endings.

I know lots of people who think well of Coleridge. I've

never been able to take his vocabulary. And Blackmur is so obscure. After all, criticism has no business being obscure—it's supposed to illuminate. And what's that fellow's name, the one who wrote the *Grammar*? Burke? I would like to read him, but his style is impossible. He says things in the most complicated language that could probably be expressed fairly easily. He seems like a fellow who lives alone and never sees anybody.

I'm thinking about getting some work done on my next book this summer.

AJA

The *Carmen Sæculare*?

WHA

No, they won't be the next. I want to do something with mines. I think I have the general approach I want.

AJA

Mines in England or mines in America?

WHA

Oh, just mines in general. I think I shall call it *Underground Life*. (*Smiling*.)

WHA

No, I don't like John Dickson Carr. He's an American, isn't he? I don't read American detective novels. I don't like H. M. or Dr. Fell. They're bad imitations of Sherlock Holmes. I think one ought to read a Faith Baldwin sometime, to see what they're like. Who do the women's stories get for heroes nowadays? Before the war they used to be explorers, but now there's so little left to explore. During the war, yes, their problems were solved by the uniform. But now? Yes, they're crazy about doctors and the nurses who marry them. Are they really so sexy? I don't think they get beyond kissing in the garden. You can use doctors away from the hospital. In England they used to have Anglo-Malayan planters. You could do that on two levels—either Somerset Maugham, or in the stories for lower-class women there would be the girl in England, and the planter would come home.

Did you see that Dewey was bidding for the Homintern vote? Yes, he vetoed a bill that would have given the magistrate power to commit a sex offender to an institution until cured and then he would have to serve out his sentence. Dewey's remarks were really very sensible. He said it would be handing the power of life and death to the magistrate and that, though of course public offenders were intolerable, a man's private life was his own affair and the law couldn't concern itself with two responsible adults who chose to misbehave privately. Yes, he's really making a play for the Homintern vote.

I went to that spy place once. All those uniforms! Anybody could tell it was a spy center. Senator Walsh was very imprudent to go. *The Post* waged a big campaign against him, published his picture with the face blocked out and the question "WHO

IS THIS?" Of course, they were out for him as an isolationist. The isolationists had to hush it up by threatening to expose Sumner Welles. That's the way those things are kept quiet—each side has too much on the other. But a public figure has to be pretty well above reproach, at least here in America. You can drink and play poker. You can even have a lady, so long as it's just one. But it's very unwise for a homosexual to be a politician. Oh, a ward politician, maybe. But they're reluctant to nominate a homosexual for public office. Generals and admirals can be queer, but public figures can't.

I don't quite like being excluded from the draft on that ground. Oh, if I'd had a heart condition or something like that, a legitimate out, I should have been delighted. But that's sort of putting you in a category with people who exhibit themselves in public places, as if when you saw a lot of naked men together, you'd leap. I should have got along quite well in the Army. From what I've seen of you, I should have excluded you.

Oh, Rilke! They just thought he was terribly incompetent and shoved him out of the way into filing work. I've spoken to a friend of his at the time—Schrecker. He was just hopeless. No, there was no idea of saving a poet involved. Even if you got a desk job with not too much work, they do keep you from nine to five, and there's no privacy. Klaus Mann wanted to go in, but it was awfully boring for the longest time for him. They had him preparing propaganda sheets until he got on *Yank*, which was more interesting. But he didn't get to Prague until after the war.

I don't know what they would have done with me. I wouldn't have had enough German for the OSS. Some kind of Intelligence probably. What I should have liked would have been a job running a town for the AMG. I have a bit of Apollo in me too. I wonder what we'll be doing in the next war.

I don't like Lord Peter Wimsey at all. I think that Poirot is a rather pale imitation of Holmes. It's all right for a detective to be a glutton—he has to have a weakness, and that isn't a dangerous one. But I don't know about vanity. Why doesn't he choose some other profession? Sherlock Holmes could have been a perfectly good chemist, but the human variables fascinated him. You can't do it for money, because then suppose the murderer paid you more to keep quiet. And you can't be a ladies' man. Either happily married or celibate. I like Inspector French to talk his cases over with his wife—that's natural. Actually neither the Holmes stories nor the Father Brown stories are very expert as problems. From that point of view, the best Holmes story is the one with the Masonic lodge, *The Valley of Fear*. And Holmes doesn't come into it until near the very end.

Sherlock Holmes was always so pleased to get on with High Society. It's one of the things that endears him to me. Bloomsbury would have been too rich for him, though.

There's no parish church in America—you have to have religion as a complement to the law. There's no rooted society. Too many summer people who don't stay. Actually, the only possible setting for an American detective story is a college. I suppose you might use the South, but it's rather decayed. I wonder why the detective story has never flourished outside England and America? The French *roman policier* is a bit different. I can see why it wouldn't flourish in Catholic countries—they have the confessional, instead. But why hasn't it taken hold in Germany? They just have translations from the English. The same thing is true of Scandinavia. They have police there, after all.

I've often thought of doing a versified detective story. But it's really an addiction, a form of escape. If the detective is involved with the pastoral setting, you can never be sure he's got the guilty ones.

Frost has something of the role Wordsworth has in England. Yes, I agree his later poems are better. Of course, remarks comparing him with old New England furniture are ridiculous. On the other hand, when it's not done absolutely well, one does find problems with bad political sentiment. I'm surprised there haven't

been more attacks on Yeats as a fascist. He's really dangerous without being direct. He once praised O'Duffy but soon wriggled out
of that like the shrewd cautious old boy he was. O'Duffy may have
started in the IRA, but ended up head of the Irish Blue Shirts.

      Yeats's last poems are, of course, competent, but they
make one feel very uncomfortable. That's what happens when
you're a virgin until you're forty as he was. It's all right to say
"prick" or "cock," but once you say something like "rod," it
sounds dirty. Everyone knows what you mean, of course, but
you're allowed to print that and not the other. You simply could
not get a line like *"Pædicabo ego vos et irrumabo"* printed today.
I'd like to write some poems like that. No, I shouldn't think of
having them published, but one wants to be able to do them. . . .

E

April 23, 1947

WHA

Come along and have a drink. What "late" works can you think of? Do you think the *Kunst der Fuge* qualifies? After all, he'd been doing that sort of thing all his life. In some ways I think the *Aeneid* is really a late work. *Bouvard et Pécuchet* is a late work. Have you read it? It's really the best thing Flaubert ever did. He may not have given it the finishing touches, though. The earlier novels are so dull. Even *L'Education Sentimentale* is quite depressing. But *Bouvard et Pécuchet* is really fun. Especially that scene where they arrive at the villa late at night and are so excited, they light the candles to look at the garden in the dark. Things keep happening. Yes, originally he may have principally been interested in the notebook, but I think he came to fall in love with his characters as he never did in his earlier works.

I think we'll go to a bar instead of up to my place. I have to get to bed early. Do you want a beer? Are you sure? I had to go to a literary club meeting at Columbia. They wanted me to speak. I said I wouldn't, but that I'd answer questions. Today, the great question seems to be, should one write poetry at all? During the thirties the question was, what *kind* of poetry should one write? Should one write poetry for the masses, for instance? But there was never any doubt whether or not one ought to write. The great question now is, what would give one pleasure? Ought one to write poetry, or fuck?

It was all rather puritanical, a bit dreary. None of the students seemed to be at all interested in technique. They'd talk about the *Four Quartets*, but nobody seemed at all interested in Eliot's imitation of Dante. Now that's a question you'd think a young poet would be quite concerned about. But they weren't.

They mostly seemed to be imitating Hart Crane. There was some Millay, some Stevens, even some me, I'm afraid. Very bad. They mostly imitated the diction. "Intricate trigonometry of the rears" was one line. I know where *that* came from. There were a few good lines. But they were all so dreadfully serious about how to achieve pleasure and whether poetry interfered with it. But they were all obviously writing like mad. They must have got the idea from James and Dewey, Hemingway and a little Kierkegaard. Kierkegaard would come in with doubts about the adequacy of poetry. That's what *les jeunes* are interested in. Most of them were queers. The "hetties" wrote like Edna St. Vincent Millay.

I'm surprised that people at Harvard should imitate Eliot as late as your time. In my day at Oxford, yes, he was extensively copied. Poetry had to be so austere. Eliot does know his meters quite thoroughly, after all. You can't catch him out about the history of English prosody. I don't think he did very much that wasn't reprinted—not after 1920 anyway. He did a great deal of humorous poetry then—stuff addressed to a friend of his. It's rather uncomfortable to read. Gray's better at comic poetry. Eliot wrote nothing *but* late poetry (*smiling*) after "Gerontion," anyway. He spoke of doing another play. I don't know whether anything's come of it.

A good bit of *The Dog Beneath the Skin* goes right into Norman Corwin's *On a Note of Triumph*—covered with shit.

AJA

Was *The Chase* your own earlier title—it was advertised under that name in *New Verse*—or did the publishers make it up?

WHA

I think it must have been the publishers. We did at first think of calling it *The Fronny* after a friend of ours. You might have a look at Anthony Collett's *The Changing Face of England*. It's a very good book but hard to come by. There are whole chunks of it embedded in *The Dog Beneath the Skin*.

Yes, "Speech from a Play" is in the *Piers Plowman*

kind of alliterative. As a matter of fact it was part of a long poem I started to do around 1930, a very long dream sequence something like the *Roman de la Rose* or *The House of Fame*. I got through Canto II before I gave it up, but some of it got included in "The Malverns." It was something like *The Age of Anxiety*—not in the eclogue form of course.

"Wafna" comes from one of the Goliardic poems. It's an expression used in connection with a hangover. No, it isn't in the *OED*.

AJA

We had such bad translations of Middle English lyrics in the Middle English course.

WHA

That's horrible. Why do they do such things? There's really no excuse for translations of Middle English. Just use a glossary. You'd want the Harrowing of Hell passus if you were doing selections from *Piers Plowman*. At Oxford, you had to take Old and Middle English, and you had your choice between fifteenth and sixteenth century literature, or nineteenth. You had to do both seventeenth and eighteenth. Seventeenth included the drama. Fifteenth-sixteenth went down to Surrey, Wyatt, even Spenser. In England everybody read the nineteenth century people. And you can't really do the nineteenth century in England without studying it on the Continent. And they ought to cut out the novels. There isn't very much you want to read in the English novel. What is that late novel of Dickens, the one with the mystic? *Edwin Drood*! That has some characteristics of "late" work. The Elizabethan novel you don't care about—a little Nashe goes a long way. And the eighteenth century novels are quite boring. I like Defoe. Not Richardson or Fielding. Richardson is simply too long. Smollett is about the only eighteenth century novelist I can read. Who are the people one likes to read in the eighteenth century? Just Pope and Johnson, and Gay. I don't really like Swift at all. The *Directions for Servants* is good. The poetry is all right, but I find *Gulliver's*

Travels one long bore. Oh, I can read the minor eighteenth century people with great pleasure. Akenside, Erasmus Darwin, Dyer. Oh yes, Young. Don't you think that's right, though, about Johnson being the prince of middlebrows? But not so much in his poetry. And those Johnsonians!

Eliot does have some strange notions. In an early essay on Dante—the one that mentions Richards—he says that our beliefs shouldn't affect our judgement of poetry. But his beliefs affect his judgement of Milton, whom he underestimates precisely because he does differ in belief from him. Now I certainly disagree with Milton's beliefs as much as Eliot does, but that doesn't put me off the poetry. As a matter of fact, I find it much easier to enjoy the poetry of writers whose beliefs I disagree with. And for all Eliot's talk about not trying to read belief from works, he does it himself, using "Ripeness is all"—Edgar's line—to adduce his thesis that the center of Shakespeare's philosophy is Stoicism. If one's going to do that kind of thing at all, you've got to take whole works and see what happens to characters expressing given opinions. Oh yes, he did it in print. I'm afraid I'm going to have to take issue with Tom about that.

I don't know why Eliot is so unfair to Milton. As a matter of fact, his unfavorable estimate prompted me to read Milton and find out how good he was. I can see the justice of some of his remarks on *Paradise Lost*, but not on *Comus*.

Actually, Eliot was giving a lecture on Milton this afternoon—not very exciting. He's thinking of a new play but wants to finish his book on culture first. The difference between us is that he thinks the Church can be more powerful in society than I think it can—that society can be made into something good. Not that he demands that statesmen be religious-minded, but he thinks they can serve that kind of interest.

I don't know why the person who arranged his appearance chose such a small hall. He could have taken a much larger one and charged very stiff prices.

EE

Eliot once gave a friend some obscene poems back in 1920 and never got them back. They think the friend's sister, who's a nun, saw them and burned them. It's all right if you know they're burned, but if you're not sure it's always worrisome.

I wonder who Eliot was thinking of when he wrote the Dante section of "Little Gidding"—Ezra Pound, or maybe Jean Verdenal. Of course, Dante was meant, but he probably had something more personal in mind. That double mirror business is just the sort of thing he'd be likely to do. I'm not a topophiliac poet. Dante is. He uses both methods of course—the *Argo* is one—but his description of the ways around Lucca is perfectly detailed, true topophilism.

There are certain differences in words between England and America. It doesn't seem that "haversack" is used in America. Do you use the word "shop" over here at all? I don't see anything more democratic about "storekeeper" as opposed to "shopkeeper." Do you think Americans used the term "gin shop," and people associated the word "shop" with that and so it got into disfavor? Harold Ross made me change "gramophone" to "phonograph" in "The Unknown Citizen." I didn't mind changing it in the least, but I felt perfectly sure everybody here would know quite well what a "gramophone" is. Harold Ross is absolutely mad. No, I don't think they would use a word like "turnery" at Harrod's— just "wooden bowls." Your friend was exaggerating. Do you know what a "goods truck" is? Just a railroad car.

Cooper is better than Scott, but you haven't said very much when you've said that. Of course, you want Disraeli. C. S. Lewis is really the best man I've seen on alliterative. *Pearl* is a great rhymed, alliterative poem. Those Viking Portables are a sinister phenomenon. I've tried to get them to let me do a Portable Firbank for them. You ought to get in about five novels—no excerpts. Let's see, what would the five be? *Santal, The Flower Beneath the Foot, Concerning the Eccentricities of Cardinal Pirelli.* . . . I sometimes think that *Vainglory* is the best of them all. Do you know who has sworn a mortal grudge against Firbank? Orville Prescott.

If I had to do a Shakespeare anthology, my selections would be both snobbish *and* representative: *The Tempest, The Winter's Tale, Love's Labour's Lost, Henry IV Parts I* and *II, Much Ado, Measure for Measure, Hamlet, Lear, Anthony and Cleopatra* —maybe *Othello* in place of *Hamlet*. I think *Twelfth Night* is a horrid play. Of the ripe plays, *Measure for Measure* is the least unpleasant. I really think Beatrice and Benedick are the best people in the comedies—even with Rosalind. And Orlando is such a stick. I'd leave *Coriolanus* to the French. I can't follow Eliot in his exalted opinion of the play. I think that Coriolanus is the most boring of Shakespeare's heroes. Macbeth is pretty dull too. I'm extremely fond of *The Winter's Tale*. Cordelia is really a silly little bitch. There are so many "No"-girls in Shakespeare's last plays. He must have acquired a special actress who could play that sort of role.

I simply cannot count. You do find people interested in such things without writing verses themselves. But a man lecturing on *Letter to Lord Byron* said it was in *ottava rima*. *And* he'd actually read the poem. He was a professor of modern literature. I haven't written much free verse. Mine is derived from Rimbaud and the Psalms.

Artists aren't as badly treated as they used to be, like Mozart. And Schubert had to use a piano at a patron's house. When somebody else wanted to play it, he simply had to go away. That sort of thing could never happen today. The good artist never has to live in extreme want. There's always some wealthy admirer who's willing to help out.

I don't know what I'm going to do next year. I think I'd like to take a rest from teaching. No, I can't go without a job completely next winter. I've undertaken to write an introduction to a book of primitive American poetry—ballads on Suzanne Degnan . . . that sort of thing. No, I didn't have time to make the selection myself. I'm thinking of getting a job in Intelligence at the State Department.

AJA

I gather Fire Island will be the scene for wild parties.

WHA

Where do you get such stories? I'm going to lead the life of a monk this summer—an absolute monk. Oh, one may drop in on a party for half an hour and eye it coldly with one's lorgnette. This must be our last drink. Fifty cents won't do you. Are you sure a dollar will be enough? (*Lending me that as I'd run out of cash.*)

April 30, 1947

WHA

Morgan Forster's coming down on the fifth of May.
He wants me to go to the Grand Canyon with him. Impossible. . . .
I'm really terribly annoyed over this teacher rating
business. It's democracy in the wrong place. It assumes that everyone's opinion is as good as everyone else's, which is simply not
true. The result is that the teacher is encouraged to clown—to be
an entertainer. But the teacher must know when he should be
boring—something necessary for students sometimes. I remember
one man at Oxford who infuriated the students by telling them
to look up things whenever they asked a question. He was lazy,
but it did them a lot of good. I remember someone at Swarthmore
who was tremendously popular with the students but was really
very bad for them. He was a "progressive," not a Marxist. If he
had been a Marxist that would have been all right—that's a discipline—but this vague "progressivism." Of course, the students
lapped it up, but it was bad for them.
    Will you have beer? I just learned that Franco has
banned *La Bohème* at the instigation of the Church. They don't
usually ban on moral grounds. You'd be surprised how many good
books still go on the *Index*. They're fairly understanding about
letting students read them though. They have Aldous Huxley on
the *Index*, quite rightly. He's been on for quite a while. Nietzsche
wouldn't be on it. I may not be a Roman Catholic, but I'm near
enough to tell what ought to go on the *Index*. If we were to make
up our own *Index*, Brahms, Shelley and Sibelius would all go on *in
toto*—and Aldous Huxley. No, I don't think Fielding should go on.
He's boring, but that's all. I shouldn't let anyone under 25 read
Whitman, and Hart Crane is dangerous for the young. And only

[57]

people who are perfectly sure of themselves should be allowed to listen to *Parsifal*. I was listening to it with Chester last evening— an amazing work. Yes, the third act.

I really think *Don Quixote* is rather boring. It goes on too long. The great thing about Sherlock Holmes, *Don Quixote* and *The Tempest* is that once you've got the idea, you know it's good. You don't have to have any poetry. The myth itself is enough. You can go on with it for yourself once you've got the point. For instance, you only have to be told about the wind- mills and you can write it up yourself. That's why there have been so many continuations of *The Tempest*—Renan . . . Browning. . . . Shakespeare really left it in a mess. Of course, you can tell with Sherlock Holmes—the writing is so absolutely worthless. But people can't see that. They think that if the myth is great, the writing must be great, which needn't be so. That's the important thing about creating a myth—its value is independent of the writing.

It's surprising that there have been so few imitations of Shakespeare. In Wordsworth, for example, you can see Milton throughout his blank verse. I don't mean imitations by his contem- poraries, where the thing was part of the general atmosphere. The Elizabethan drama was more or less one piece up to 1642. Oh, Otway! He's very dull—impossible to read. And it isn't that Shake- speare doesn't have a definite style—you can pick out his contribu- tions to *Henry VIII* and *Two Noble Kinsmen* from those of Beau- mont and Fletcher.

No, I don't think "Our revels now are ended" is such a purple patch or the one passage that one would want to take as the high point of Shakespeare's art. It's all right, but *Antony and Cleopatra* is much better poetry. It has to be; they've nothing else to live on. No, I don't think that the greater the theme the greater the poetry, all other things being equal. Yes, the words are absolute- ly vital to the masque. But afterwards, when Prospero hears of Caliban making mischief, you could tell the story any which way and it would be just as effective. What he's saying is simply, "I want to die." He's very tired and doesn't want to be bothered.

Where the poetry is good, it's not vital to the myth—it isn't essential as it is in *Antony and Cleopatra*. Myth and poetry exist independently of each other. *Don Quixote* is the only really Christian myth. You find a trace of it in *Li'l Abner* in the *Daily Mirror*. Abner's always trying to do someone a good turn, and it never works out. *Superman* and *Little Orphan Annie* ought to be on the *Index*. Henry Miller, certainly. Yes, Thomas Wolfe . . . and Carl Sandburg—the prose is all right, but not the poetry.

My introduction to the Tennyson anthology seems to have created a great stir in England, because I said that Tennyson was stupid. Desmond MacCarthy took me to task severely—he's the Grand Old Man of English criticism—something like Edmund Wilson in this country, but a little older. So now the publishers over there are advertising it as "that controversial volume." They didn't stop to think that if I didn't like Tennyson I shouldn't have bothered to write an introduction at all.

You know, I've come to the conclusion that W. S. Gilbert was really a horrible, wild old queen. I don't see how they can play *Iolanthe* in the United States with "fairy" meaning what it does. And that dialogue with the Guardsman where she says, "You're a fine fellow, sir," and he says (*deeper voice*), "I am generally admired."

This will have to be our last drink. Before you go I want you to see this paper. (*Pulling out an announcement for the United Jewish Appeal.*) Not that. (*Pulls out the exam sheet for "marking" teachers.*) There, isn't it awful? Now if I could only get fifty of the students to say they caught the teacher groping, that would be something.

May 3, 1947

I WENT into a little bar near the Waverly Theater and started drinking beer and reading An Oxford Tragedy, *when I spotted* WHA *dining in solitude in the back room. I joined him, and he seemed to make no objection.*

WHA

You don't like Betjeman? That's really my world—bicycles and harmoniums. You don't go on bicycle trips now, the way they did. The real thing is the Church. It's what separates England from the Continent as well as from America. Oh yes, Oxford fits right in. You know the great distinction between the hats of the clergy? Broad Churchmen wear hats with speckled brims, Low Churchmen wear funny-looking hats with things hanging round the sides, and High Churchmen wear ordinary black felt hats. I'm surprised you like Trollope. Do you really understand over here the society he's describing? Betjeman is really a minor poet, of course.

May 7, 1947

WE had been discussing my checking the syllabification of WHA'S *verse.*

WHA

I decided not to do any correcting of the earlier syllabic pieces. After all, they're all in print. I shouldn't go back on them. That was a detestable habit of George Moore's—he kept revising his works. But you're absolutely like Iago. I'm never going to be able to let you go. I've never met anyone outside yourself who makes any effort to count—to see what one's doing. Even Ted Spencer, who after all is quite good, seems to have no conception of that kind of prosodic problem. Either you get people who make the most idiotic suggestions, or else they assume that you're allowed to do anything. There's so little awareness of definite form in America. What a contrast to the eighteenth century, when they jumped on you for putting a cæsura in the wrong place. Of course, that can go too far.

You know, the basic English line has four stresses. The language seems to go by twos and fours—that's why you have to say "a *fuck*ing *day*." French works on an entirely different principle. I wonder whether they have anything like it in German.

In the *Beowulf* line you keep hearing the base in blank verse—it seems so silly to talk about "iambic pentameter"—but most of the lines really only have four stresses. For instance, "in *hide*ous *ru*in and com*bus*tion *down*." Yes, the pace is slower than Skelton's But when you get down to it, what is the prosodic accent without the rhetorical?

I can't make anything of the sing-song in Greek.

[61]

Where do they get the idea of the conflict between accent and
quantity in the first hemistich of Latin hexameter? Who originated
the theory? In pronouncing Latin verse one ought to follow the
Italian practice in the matter. After all, they're the nearest.
English produces spondees without effort. For an inflected language it's a real achievement. The surrounding structure
helps you scan "Coursed · down · on their con · catenation" cor-
rectly, otherwise the temptation would be to scan "Coursed ·
down on their · concate · nation." You have two traditions in English prosody: the foot and the simple accent-unstressed syllable
combination—the type of thing you find in Hopkins. Quantitative
verse isn't necessarily written accentually. In Surrey and Wyatt
you can see they're simply counting syllables. That's why you
have what looks like roughness in the prosody.

They were trying to make the accents coincide there.
But that's not always the theory. For instance, Campion is just
interested in the quantity—the accent is there though, even if he
won't admit it. Bridges did work where the quantity and accent
didn't coincide.

It's amazing how little students know about prosody.
When you teach a college class, you find they read either as
straight prose, or as deadly monotonous beat as in *Gorboduc*. At
the beginning—in *Gorboduc*— the Elizabethan dramatists may have
started off with the idea of doing a strict five-beat line, but as they
went on, they found that too cramping and made increasing use
of the line with four stresses—though, of course, they might keep
the line with ten syllables. I find Saintsbury's *History of English
Prosody* quite exasperating at times. Bridges's *Milton's Prosody*
does recognize less than five accents. Saintsbury is the best writer
on prosody, though. Even when writers seem to follow the foot
system, they don't ignore stress.

Did you see *The Importance of Being Earnest?* It's an
extraordinarily good play. It's about nothing at all, which is what

makes it so good. *Lady Windermere's Fan* has some social refer-
ence, which makes it not so good. But *The Importance of Being
Earnest* isn't a bit dated. The trouble with Shaw's plays is that
they're all brain and no body, which isn't good for the stage. There
may not be any body in *Earnest*, but at least there are clothes. Obviously you have to see it—you can't just read it. Just as, on the
other hand, *Lear* won't do on the stage. Wilde, after all, is important not as a writer—he couldn't write at all—but as a behaver.
Still he did say some very acute things. "After twenty years of
romantic love a woman looks like a ruin. After twenty years of
marriage she looks like a public building." Now that's absolutely
right. It's very good. And his remark on his deathbed, "I am dying
as I have lived—beyond my means."

I don't think you could call the Chaplin story a myth
because you couldn't separate it from the man who acts it. It's
farce. Who are the great masters of farce I've seen? Chaplin,
Grock, Marie Lloyd and Groucho Marx. Groucho is really the
only one of the brothers with brains. Some of his cracks are marvelous. No, he isn't really so good as Chaplin.

I should really like very much to meet the man who
draws *Li'l Abner*. I think that you can set as a criterion for the
good comic strip is that it gets better in bulk. The drawing in
Terry and the Pirates is very good indeed, but it doesn't improve
in bulk, and the only reason to keep reading it is because the hero
looks so pretty. *Gasoline Alley* might be a real myth. It's the completely mediocre person growing up. But it couldn't be a myth
unless it included everything. Yes, you should see him masturbat-
ing on the doorstep one minute and going to church the next.

Do you know who Bradford is? He's an Anglican
clergyman who wrote some poems early in the twentieth century
with a good bit about beautiful choirboys. One of the reviewers
called attention to it as evidence of homosexuality, but nobody did
anything about it. Then there's another Anglican clergyman

named Cottam who wrote a poem about a boy: "His neck was of a lovely brown / 'Twas even lovelier lower down." I've heard Cottam preach. Nothing happened to either of them. They stayed clergymen. The Anglican Church is a wonderful place if you need protection. I don't see how Bradford could have written in quite the way he did if he'd actually gone to bed with boys. I don't think Whitman actually went to bed with boys either. Oh, Bradford is a modernist—he lectures to his congregation in the Fens on Einstein.

WHA

Did you see that Mary McCarthy has joined the anti-Homintern? Yes, she talks about "those who are unfortunately afflicted with the burden of bisexuality." It isn't her late husband, it's her present husband. What do you know about him? Ted Spencer introduced me to Broadwater once, but he didn't seem to be anything unusual. Why do you suppose she married him? And she isn't really important enough for him to get any prestige out of being her husband. As a matter of fact, it's the way for him to lose what individuality he's got—to be known simply as Mary McCarthy's husband. I don't quite see what he could expect from marrying her. She isn't the sort of person who can make people happy, and when you get married you do, after all, expect some amount of happiness.

Bunny Wilson must be a rather difficult person to live with, too. His new wife is a very nice, quiet person. Women should be quiet. When people are talking, they ought to retire to the kitchen. Unfortunately, over here there isn't any division between the kitchen and the rest of the house. Of course, it's no good when women keep silently disapproving. But they can be quiet and nice at the same time. It's awful when they keep on talking without having anything to say. Over here, though, the men are so dull it's sometimes a relief when a woman talks. It's all right for a woman to talk when she's really witty. But even then one has the impression she's really very unhappy and is being witty, not out of good spirits, but to cheer herself up. That leaves a very painful impression indeed. One feels so sorry that one can't enjoy the wit. No, I don't like it when women are nasty. Women are really supposed to be much nicer than men. That's what they're here for. Women

[65]

shouldn't be talked to on intellectual subjects because if they like you, they'll agree without having any real opinions of their own. Oh, they are fun to talk gossip with. A few have real minds, but they usually make one feel uncomfortable. Maiden aunts must be very pious and go to church regularly. No, I've never had to live with one for an extended period.

People are really brought up better in England than in America. You must acquire a social manner, learn how to pass the tea cups round gracefully. If you just say, "My, what a lovely hat you have on today," and roll your eyes a little, they're delighted. You can't be rude unless you're fearfully grand. It takes a lot to bring it off.

I told him about asking the Whatmoughs whether they'd had a nice summer in 1939.

_{WHA}

Oh no, you shouldn't have done that—that was really tactless. Ted Spencer told me you were a little unworldly.

Twelfth Night is really a very nasty play. Everybody reads it in school and says, "How lovely" because it has no sex in it. If it were a frankly unpleasant play, it would be all right. But he started out to write a pleasant play like *As You Like It* and was trapped by his own convention. Oh yes, it's well written all right, but I don't like it.

Yes, I suppose if you weighed per volume, Browne would have a very large number of words. I don't think Burton would have more—so much of his variety comes though his use of Latin.

May 17, 1947

I don't think that "*Le Bateau Ivre*" is Rimbaud's best work. So many people have been influenced by it when there are so many other, better things he's done that they could have profited from. I think I read "*Les Assis*" first by itself. No, I don't think one would be inclined to take it as satirical. Verlaine himself wasn't so good. Who did he include in *Les Poètes Maudits*? Was Mallarmé older than he?

Most people don't realize that Churchill is a comparatively decadent follower of Burke in his oratory. That's why they think he's better than he is. But when you compare his speeches with those of other politicians—except Hitler, of course—well. . . . Hitler had this very effective trick of beginning his speeches slowly and getting more and more excited as he went on.

Some Siamese cats are impossible because they keep continually crying. I'd rather have a tom. You know, they have a rugged time of it trying to service so many ladies. A friend's was looking seedy. When he called the vet, the vet just laughed and said the cat would be fine once the rutting season was over. Cats will not let you work. They keep jumping all over you, try to attract your attention and just make a nuisance of themselves.

I'm going to do, if I can, a guidebook to England. I shall do it in collaboration with Betjeman. I don't know how much material is available at the New York Public Library. I shall create a furor with the things I shall advise people not to read. Oh no, it's not going to be just a Bædeker—it's going to be a general introduction to the people and the country. Yes, I hope to do the Firbank. I want to use the word "Homintern."

Orville Prescott will be furious over the Betjeman and

the Firbank. They let Adams do his "Treasure Chest" page to ease
the blow. But the *New York Times Book Review* people are such
cowards. I believe in anonymous reviewing—a paper shouldn't let
in a review just because it's by somebody famous. It ought to insist
that a review be up to its standards—which I admit are really
rather low. I don't suppose you can write a review every day and
be any good. Prescott does it four times a week. Can you think of
anyone who does it oftener? I suppose they do let someone else do
the review sometimes. It was hard enough reviewing detective
stories which I did one time for the *Daily Telegraph*. Eventually,
you ran out of things to say. I had to read about seven and then
select the three or four that I wanted to write about. As a matter
of fact, I like the way the *Saturday Review* does them with little
boxes for the plot, theme, comment, etc. That's how they ought
to be done. No, you couldn't tell the reviewers not to disclose the
plot of *The Age of Anxiety*—it just isn't done. You might seal up
some pages the way they do in mysteries.

Oh yes, I've seen these Cadmus drawings. I don't think
they're as good as the frankly pornographic ones. He's doing a
horribly frightening set of pictures now—the Seven Deadly Sins.
They're very good, but I don't like them. Sloth is the best. He
hasn't done Lust yet, and that's going to present difficulties. It
will have to go in a church—that's the only place for it—perhaps
St. Mary's in Northampton—in England. Oh, it could be put in a
dark chapel. It's amazing how loathsome he makes his people. He
and his friends all derive from Breughel. Personally Paul is an extremely quiet person—very faithful in his relationships.

WHA

Ah, nice to see you. We've got a cat—Siamese. Come here, Bastien. Now there are some people who think all you have to do is give a cat a saucer of milk now and then, and it's got enough to live on. That's not true at all—it needs meat. I suppose the cat manages to get out and eat something when it's only given milk. I feed mine liver and fish, two meals a day. It's always making a racket. No, you're not going to get any more to eat so you might as well keep quiet. I couldn't come back to town by train as the cat would have been too upset. I had to come back by car. Yes, it likes being stroked, but what it really likes is being slapped on the hindquarters. (*Suiting the action to the word.*) I hope it doesn't shit on the floor.

I'm annoyed about the article for *Harpers Bazaar.* I had to get it off in three days and I couldn't get hold of the quotations I wanted. I like a little potboiler—two or three pages—I'm doing for *House and Garden* much better. It's on "Why I Like Cold Weather." The one thing I read this summer that really impressed me was Fitzgerald's *Tender Is the Night.* I think it's even better than *The Great Gatsby.* Yes, it's a later work. One book that really shocked me was *The Bostonians.* The Lesbianism is so marked. I'm amazed there wasn't any outcry. James himself said, "The book is much odder than they think."

Oh, Verena is simply trade. Of course, he'd be hard on Olive just because he sees himself in her. He may not approve of Ransom altogether, but he obviously admires him very much.

I suggest some of the novellas—they're really his best work. Let's see, there's *The Pupil*—that's a queer one—*The Aspern Papers, In the Cage, Death of the Lion, The Beast in the Jungle.* No,

[69]

I'm afraid James's plays really won't do. The characters are too intelligent, and there isn't any part for a great actress.

Yes, "Law Like Love" was written over here. I don't think that you could tell which works in *Another Time* were written here. After all, a good many of them weren't published in magazines. "Where Do They Come From" is like "Oxford" and "Casino." They're not syllabic. "The Capital" was written in Europe. After all, there aren't many farm boys in Manhattan. The first poem I wrote over here was the one on Yeats's death. No, I wasn't thinking of Birmingham in Stage IV, though it's true that some of the biggest red sandstone deposits are in the vicinity.

There's a book I'd like you to see—Nora Kershaw's *Anglo-Saxon and Norse Poems*. Here's a companion volume. Where did I put it? Someone must have borrowed it. I just got back last night and don't know where anything is. (*Getting down on his hands and knees and creeping behind the couch.*) Oh, here it is. You see Rosetta's song in seven-syllable lines is imitated from the *Sonatorrek* in—let me see—(*turning to page*) yes, Kvithuháttr. I don't keep the alliteration of three and four syllables in the half-lines—I was trying something else. There are some lines with more than one cæsura—for instance, "To elude Him, to lie to Him, yet His love observes." I think you got all the alliterative devices.

AJA

In Malin's lyric in Stage IV, you have to make "at the scratch" work into a run-on line.

WHA

Oh, that's all right—it's a lyric meter. You pronounce the word "*hepato · scopists*" like "*photo · grapher.*" (*Looking it up in the OED and finding he was right.*) I tried to do something with "To the Cross or to *Clarté* or to Common Sense"—but it'll have to stay that way. The main sources for Quant's speech in Stage III were Baudelaire and Botticelli's *Primavera*.

AJA

In "heavy like us" you could save the alliteration by

syncopating the "ke" and positing the "k" as the fourth alliterating letter, the reverse of what you sometimes do in nouns where an intravocalic consonant can be put with the preceding non-alliterating syllable.

WHA

I know, but the reader has been trained to expect the initial vowel as the alliterating element. Besides, doesn't *Beowulf* sometimes alliterate in four places? I've got to go out now to see if the new Michael Innes is in the lending library.

WHA

Let's go out, shall we? Oh yes, I still go to that little place in spite of the television set. The food is so good. No, they don't really have sole here. It's some kind of flounder, I think. They only have it in Europe. And the vegetables don't taste right. They ought to eat more Brussels sprouts here. Oh, broccoli does very well frozen.

I have to give a talk on Yeats before the MLA in Detroit. You know, the more I read him, the less I like him. Take that phrase, "that gong-tormented sea." When you first read it, it sounds wonderful, but when you come to examine it, it's simply nonsense. It's from the second Byzantium poem. No, you can't say it's vibrating because the gong would have to be ringing in the sea and that won't do. The gongs obviously come from some kind of procession on land. No, "dolphin-torn" is all right for a pathetic fallacy, but "gong-tormented" won't do. No, it won't do at all. He was a horrible old man.

No, I couldn't launch an open attack on him. This is supposed to be some kind of celebration, after all. I wouldn't mind his crazy mythology if he took it more seriously. And all right, I wouldn't mind it's being a hoax if he tipped us a wink at the end. I like *really* crazy people like Rilke, yes, and D. H. Lawrence. And in Goethe you know the machinery is just machinery. That's all right too. And after all, you are perfectly certain that Goethe was quite convinced of his beliefs and held them strongly. But with Yeats, that's not at all true. And, of course, his people weren't related to the Butlers at all.

I'm doing a selected edition of Pope. Some of the lines are wonderful—"Bare the mean Heart that lurks beneath a Star." You know it's the Garter, and yet somehow it isn't. And you know that wonderful remark that Johnson made about his grotto—"Pope's excavation was requisite as an entrance to his garden, and, as some men try to be proud of their defects, he extracted an ornament from an inconvenience, and vanity produced a grotto where necessity enforced a passage."

The *Essay on Criticism* is dull. (*He started making cat's cradles.*) That line which runs "And beastly Skelton Heads of Houses quote." I'm sure he must have meant heads of colleges. I don't think the squires would have known Skelton.

No, I don't like Toye's book on Rossini any better than I do his Verdi. He doesn't give you any sense of the composer's background, of what his contemporaries were doing in opera. Did you see *Werther*? There were only two tunes in the opera—a sad tune and a gay tune—but it was rather nice. Verdi never wrote a good overture except the one to *La Forza*. And he wasn't interested in ballet music, so his is rather dull—for instance, *Aida*.

Have you read C. S. Lewis's book on miracles? All these modern people who tell you you shouldn't anthropomorphize God. Lewis tells about one person who was told God was a Perfect Substance, and this always led her to envision Him as a vast junket. No, you're much better off envisioning God in the form of your father. After all, your father is the person you think of as being all-wise, all-powerful, all-good and caring for you. Oh, of course, when you get older you realize that your father isn't so perfect, but he still is your first image of what is good, and it's the most satisfactory analogue to God for a child.

WHA

I'm to do an anthology of Greek literature. What do you think I should put in? I'm having the sixth and twenty-second book of the *Iliad*, the whole *Oresteia* (for tragedy), either the *Clouds*, the *Birds*, or the *Frogs* (for comedy), the Sicilian expedition and the Melian dialogue from Thucydides—oh, did Hobbes do a translation?—the story of Polycrates from Herodotus, all the fragments of Heraclitus, Hippocrates' *Airs, Waters, and Places*, parallel passages from the *Physics* and *Metaphysics* about the unmoved mover, the *Timæus* and the *Symposium* of Plato and the *Poetics*, I think. I don't know what to do about political ideas. Yes, maybe the *Laws* would be a good idea. Then I want a short Christian section: the beginning of John (I think you ought to pronounce "and without Him was not any thing made that *was* made," don't you think? Not "any thing made that was *made*), the Romans, the thirteenth Corinthians and finish up with the Athanasian Creed. I wish you'd look through the Apostolic Fathers and see if you can dig up anything interesting. I shall need your advice in general about the thing.

AJA

I think you have a very good program without me.

WHA

I can't be too hard on the Greeks. If I said, "They're awful, don't read them," what would be the point of the anthology? No, the people I really like are Atomists. They influenced Thucydides a great deal. So did the medical people. After all, when you ask what are the Greeks outstanding for, it's surely for their use of hypotheses in every subject. I shall have to have some Euclid, I guess. The *Elements* probably. I'd like to put in a little Oppian.

What do you know about the history of the text of Aeschylus—what manuscripts they've been preserved in? It's that sort of thing that makes me feel so in awe of Greek scholars. Isocrates reminds me of John Dewey. He's a mediocrity who's usu-

ally right whereas Plato is a man of genius who's always wrong.
I think people are wrong in opposing Plato to Aristotle. Plato's
real rival is Thucydides, who unlike both and following Pericles,
did not deify the state but regarded it as a convenience.

You know, it's surprising how few imitations, real imitations, of Greek there are in Englsh. There are really only two—
Samson Agonistes and *The Wreck of the Deutschland.* Oh yes,
Hopkins really. gets the Pindaric use of language and the form—
the initial invocation, what happens to the nuns corresponds to
the myth, and so on. The earlier people never really got the point
of Pindar. I think you can find stichomythy in Senecan drama.
The man who said Socratic dialogue came from the question and
answer in Eleusinian initiation rites was perfectly right. So does
stichomythy in tragedy, which also involves question and answer.
Yes, you're right, Landor's epigrams do represent a further use of
Greek models. And Browning is another one. Why don't imita-
tors of Milton imitate the one really original element of his style,
his syntax?

When reading Mörike one gets the impression that he's
really a very nice man. Oh yes, Lancelot Andrewes is very good
indeed, and not at all known. People read his *Meditations* much
more than his *Sermons.* I'm very fond of Jeremy Taylor. I adore
the Scottish Psalter with its strange meters and its fantastic gram-
matical inversions.

Oh, yes. I like Boswell much better than Eckermann.
You could see Goethe deliberately saying things to shock Eckermann, and Eckermann going home and spending a long time thinking over what the Master had said. Have you seen the Ben Shahn
exhibition? He's really quite good.

AJA

If you'll forgive me for saying so, you seem much
cheerier than last time.

WHA

(*Taken aback.*) Oh? When was that? It was probably
the hot weather.

WHA

(*To the cat.*) Come here, dear. Look what I have for you. (*To me.*) I got a new crapper for him. I hope he uses it. We'll have to lock him in the bathroom while this food is being prepared, otherwise there'll be no holding him. He's an awfully queer cat, I'm sure.

I told you about my doing an opera with Stravinsky, didn't I? Oh, I didn't? I thought I had. Boosey and Hawkes called up and asked me if I wanted to do it. It's a great honor. It will be given at the Metropolitan. He's doing a mass now. The last things he did for voices were the *Symphonie de Psaumes* and *Oedipus Rex* in the early thirties. Boosey and Hawkes pay him $25,000 a year. I hope they'll pay me to fly out to the coast and confer with him sometime in January. It will be done before April. It's to be on Hogarth's *Rake's Progress*. Evidently Stravinsky's been thinking about it a long time.

I hope he has some ideas about the plot because before I can do any work on it, I'll have to have a plot. There are to be seven characters—three men and three women, in addition to the hero. I think I'd like to connect it with the Seven Deadly Sins. The hero, of course, will represent Pride, the young girl Lust, I think. The rich old woman will be Avarice, the false friend Anger, the servant Envy and so on. Instead of the gambling scene I'd like to have a cockfight, but I don't know whether I can get away with it. Perhaps the crowd could be standing round concealing the cocks from view and the orchestra could imitate the noises they would make in fighting. Or perhaps we could use marionettes. I don't know. The final scene in the madhouse where the hero is crowned as Lucifer I'd like to treat as a coronation service. He ought to be anointed with a chamber pot, but I don't know whether people would stand for that. But piss is the only proper chrism. It has to be done in eighteenth century style.

Oh yes, there will be prose passages. The standard meter will have to be heroic couplets. In the choruses, where the words aren't so important, I can fool around with fancier meters. The girl turns up in the final scenes. I don't know what I'm going to do with her. The duets ought to be got out of the way earlier. In the last scene I want the hero to stand alone. But what *am* I going to do with the plot? Stravinsky's supposed to be very easy to work with. It will be a wonderful experience. I'm so excited about it. No, I don't think there will be any friction. He'll tell me where he wants long lines for his music, and I can let him know when a scene seems insufficiently dramatic. Yes, it's a special challenge to fit the words in properly. No, I don't think it will necessarily be suitable for separate publication, though if anything should come out of it, I shouldn't mind.

The English Church was so Erastian during the eighteenth century. Almost all the bishops were Deists or Unitarians. The C of E was a great accident. Henry didn't care a straw about reforming doctrine. It could still be Catholic in doctrine. Oh yes, plenty of Anglicans still believe in Purgatory. They may find loopholes, but some of them simply say they don't accept the Article—against the Romish doctrine of Purgatory. But, though there's nothing against Prayers for the Dead, they don't claim that the Prayers are bound to get them any reduction in punishment. Even the Roman church now simply says that God can listen to the Prayers if He wants to.

The English Catholic liturgy, the old Sarum Use, was much more spikey than the Continental equivalents. Oh, the Church is still allowed to receive legacies from the dead. I'm sure of it. I don't think the Statute of Mortmain still applies. The American Prayer Book is quite like the English, except they leave out the sentence, "with my body I thee worship" from the Marriage Service.

Yes, I have thought how the churches can be brought together. Where's the only place to meet that would be satisfactory to all of them? Jerusalem, obviously. That's a holy place for everybody. The "*filioque*" clause wouldn't make much difference. After all, the Greek church objected to that largely because the decision was taken without their having been consulted. There hasn't been any great amount of controversial literature on the subject. Of course, they'd be allowed not to insert the clause if they didn't want it. All the Western churches have the clause— even the Lutheran. The Nicene Creed would be the basis for intercommunion. You know the Anglicans can already communicate with the Greek Orthodox as well as with the Swedish church. There could be some equitable agreement for not raiding each other, though that would be a difficult point. Of course, you couldn't communicate with Unitarians.

There is a move on, largely among Low Churchmen, to initiate intercommunion in the other direction—with the Presbyterians. Much as I dislike that old ass Bishop Manning, he did have a point when he said there are some things on which we must not yield. They were giving away practically everything to the Presbyterians. What keeps the churches apart now is more a matter of bad manners than of actual doctrinal difference. I wonder how much the Pope is a prisoner of the Cardinals. If he should go counter to the general line—for instance, if he were to condemn Franco—would the people who hold the purse strings step in and say, "Now you're going too far. You have to pull in your horns"?

In England I used to believe very strongly in Disestablishment, but after seeing its fruits over here, I'm not so sure. When Convocation last revised the Prayer Book, Parliament threw it out as being too Papistical. I don't see why the Non-Conformists in Commons should vote on a Church bill. You'd think they'd abstain. After all, they don't attend. No, they don't think they can force a Presbyterian. But they're lower than Low Churchmen inside the church, and they're determined to keep out Popery. Do the French really subsidize all religions, I wonder?

I never really fell in love until I was thirty-two, and then Venus found her prey! When I was very young, I used to go with people of my own class. Chester was the first person I met who was both sexually attractive and not a bore. With Christopher, well, one could send the girls out of the room and discuss Proust. Oh, one made a fuss of course, but nothing serious. One time Denny Foutts—he was a famous courtesan of the period—was being kept by Lord Tredegar, and Wells came to the house for dinner and liked Denny very much. So much that he invited him to a luncheon which he was giving to reconcile four of his mistresses. Well, in the first place, Denny had to have some teeth taken care of, so he arrived an hour late. That was bad enough to begin with. The only thing all of them seemed to have in common was anti-Fascism. So they began condemning Hitler's concentration camps and saying how horrible they were. And Denny said, "Oh, they aren't so bad. I was in one once for two years." They all became very interested and excited and asked how it had happened. Denny answered, "Homosexuality," and the luncheon simply broke up. Wells is really "anti"—he says they're sick people. The Communists are very severe. In fact, they used to trap our boys at the Embassy by sending round lovelies to proposition them. Now unless you're really ravishingly beautiful, you know you're not very likely to receive advances from people without some ulterior motive. You've simply got to learn to say, "No thank you, dear, I'd love to but. . . ." Because once they get something on you they can make it very unpleasant, as they did for a number of people at the Embassy. An ambassador can never really get away with doing anything. Inverchapel never really does anything. This business of his with the Iowa boy is perfectly chaste, because even over here you can imagine how much the *Chicago Tribune* would like to get his scalp. But if they approached the boy with offers of money—if he'd talk —the boy wouldn't even know what they meant. Oh yes, he likes his job very well.

During the war the ONI seemed to have nothing to do except chase down homosexuals in the Navy. The Army Intelligence never seemed to bother. After all, with the war some rather odd characters drifted into the Army. It's incredible the pains the Navy took to catch them. There's a very amusing story about how the ONI caught a British naval officer living with an American sailor. It shows the difference between the British and American attitudes. They informed the Admiralty and said, "We've taken care of the sailor—you can take care of the officer." The Admiralty wired back, "Has there been any scandal?" — "No." — "Then what's all the fuss about?" The Americans were terribly shocked. But the British don't worry about it at all. There's a good deal of it on board ships. The ONI can't do anything to civilians, of course, but they do watch queer bars more than you think to see which sailors frequent them. When they catch one they either kick him out or make him tell on the ones he's slept with. And it doesn't do any good for him to say he hasn't slept with anyone—they won't accept that as an excuse. And if they find he's been holding out on them—out he goes. They set very elaborate traps. Sailors obviously can't blackmail civilians, but they roll them.

The reasons Americans pretend so hard about the subject is that America is really a very queer country. I've come to the conclusion that it's wrong to be queer, but that's a long story. Oh, the reasons why are comparatively simple. In the first place, all homosexual acts are acts of envy. In the second, the more you're involved with someone, the more trouble arises, and affection shouldn't result in that. It shows something's wrong somewhere.

I've been reading *This Side of Paradise*. Chester gave it to me. Those long conversations between the Princeton man and his girl. One simply can't believe that he cared for her in the least. All American writing gives the impression that Americans really don't care for girls at all. What the American male really wants is two things: he wants to be blown by a stranger while reading a newspaper and he wants to be fucked by his buddy when he's

drunk. Everything else is society. Europeans really can be heterosexual. Even in Kafka. All right, Kafka may have something up his
sleeve, but you still feel that he genuinely wants to go to bed with
the woman.

I really find it hard now to pretend an interest I don't
feel. And I can't stay up till two and three in the morning. I feel
very guilty now about encouraging people to think I care more
than I do about them. I don't care for the excitement of the chase
one little bit. What I would really like would be a brothel where
you simply go in, pay your money, and go home at a reasonable
hour without any misunderstandings on either side. In Berlin I
lived next door to a brothel, and I didn't have to wait till late at
night. I could go in at nine o'clock and get to bed by midnight. I'm
afraid Miss God insists that I go to bed early.

Sexual fidelity is more important in a homosexual relationship than in any other. In other relationships there are a variety
of ties. But here, fidelity is the only bond. Anyway, Chester has
no right to be jealous—he was the one who left me—not I him. But
still he can be awfully difficult about these things. I wish Chester
had a contemporary who would keep him away from this staying up till four in the morning. It's all right on weekends, but
when it goes on in the middle of the week, that's too much. He
needs a friend who doesn't like music.

I used to think that the fear of rejection was Jewish.
Now I'm beginning to think it's an American characteristic. I was
always so amazed at Chester's laying himself out to be nice to
people about whom he was quite contemptuous behind their backs.
Oh, *you* manifest the same characteristics negatively.

Do you share the general American shock over the
European attitude that the lower classes simply ought to go to
bed when asked? Chester was horribly shocked when I told him
I felt that way. You know, when the Admirals were objecting to
Churchill's proposal to invade Norway, saying that it wasn't in the
tradition of the British Navy, Churchill said, "The British Navy

G

has only three traditions—rum, mutiny and sodomy."

I thought we'd have another drink, but I see that it's ten to seven and I've got to run. First I've got to buy a bottle of gin. (*Putting his glasses on to look at the name on the bottle.*) Oh, do you think Dixie Belle is good? Well, let's have some of that then.

Oh, I never take anæsthetics when I'm having my teeth drilled. I guess I had too Spartan a home as a boy. Going to the dentist's is like going to the barber to get one's hair cut—a terrible waste of time and money. I have my hair cut as seldom as possible.

Halloween 1947

WHA

I'm glad you showed up because there's something I want you to do for me: a chronological table of Greek literature.

I think if one's a Communist and being investigated by a Congressional Committee one ought to say so. (*Apropos of the House Committee on Un-American Activities' investigation of the movie industry*.) After all, they're going to lose their jobs anyway and might as well get the credit for being courageous. Oh, of course, the Committee has no right to ask any such question. And if you're not a Communist, you ought not to answer. But if you are. . . . And as for Negroes, I simply can't understand why every Negro isn't a Communist. It's the only system that holds out any hope for them.

I don't know that Brecht is still a Communist. He had some very severe things to say about them when the war broke out. I don't think he ever actually took out a party card. Writers are pretty careful about that sort of thing.

I think a few bombs would wipe out any pro-Russian sentiment in New York. When you're first bombed, your first reaction is one of anger—of wanting to hit back. But when it goes on day after day, you get numb—your only thought is, "Please let it stop." I can't understand why the Germans didn't keep up the bombing of London. If they'd gone on another month, England would have given in, Churchill or no Churchill.

The great difficulty for us with regard to Greek thinking is that they had no idea of the importance of freedom of choice. I don't see how Plato reconciled the Demiurge of the *Timæus* with the vision of Er at the end of *The Republic* with its system of rewards and punishments. How far did he believe in either of them?

AJA

In the Stoics and Epicureans, it's the other way round
—all will and no environment.

WHA

Yes, classical Greek culture was past its peak. That horrible old Marcus Aurelius. The question of existence didn't seem
to bother the Greeks at all—and it's so important for Christians.
That's why it's so hard to answer the question, what did the Greeks
believe? I'm not talking about the Roman period when it was generally held that the gods were allegorical personifications, but
when people were serious about following the ritual. And yet they
didn't seem to care whether their deities existed or not, or about
the details of their careers. Now Americans would care terribly
if someone turned up with absolute and incontrovertible proof
that George Washington never existed. And those interminable
Athenian prosecutions!

AJA

What does it remind one of? France . . . the Dreyfus
case . . . or perhaps Sacco and Vanzetti?

WHA

No, no. The Dreyfus case is right. That perpetual
French atmosphere of intrigue. You cannot have democratic gov-
ernment with more than three parties. That's the trouble with
France—that was the trouble with the Weimar Republic.

AJA

I suppose you are in favor of the repeal of proportional
representation?

WHA

Absolutely. It's a very great mistake and should never
have been passed in the first place. I shall gladly vote against it.

It may be necessary to interpret dogmas in different
ways for different periods, but the dogmas remain the same. I don't
think that Aristotle really liked poetry. I think he had a wife who
liked to go to the theater and came home raving about the latest
play, so that finally he felt that he had to do something about the

subject to prove that he could if he set his mind to it. His description suggests that he knew only Sophocles.

Yes, I liked *Titus Groan* very much. I was sorry that it made so little splash over here. It's wonderfully anal. All those old rooms filled with junk. The Americans are violently oral. Do you know George Thingummy? He was over here on a visit and wrote an article about American civilization for *Life* with that theme. He said that was why Americans were always more ready to give money than food. They were always afraid they'd starve. *Life* got some very angry letters about that. And the important thing in America is not to have money, but to have had it—to be worthy of having mother's love.

AJA

Don't you think that may be a cultural lag from the prairie days when food was more important than money?

WHA

No, the oral business is more important. That's why in America the mother is all-important and the father has no position at all—isn't respected in the least. Even the American passion for laxatives can be explained as an oral manifestation. They want to get rid of any unpleasantness taken in through the mouth.

Even in women's clubs, they don't really respect the lecturer because next week they'll turn round and approve just as cordially the next speaker whose views may be the exact opposite.

For an Englishman coming over here to teach, the rudeness of the students is quite shocking. After all, he is more or less in the position of a father. The psychological background of American students doesn't teach them obedience to a father image, which is too bad. It isn't that they shouldn't eventually find out the limitations of the father substitute and eventually discard him —that's quite as it should be. But they begin with the idea that they are the important ones to be pleased—not taught—and that their untutored reactions should be the final judgement on their instructor. They're so disobedient because that's the way they've been brought up.

GG

WHA

I'm just back from California. Stravinsky was extraordinarily nice. I played duets with him on the piano. Some of the fugal parts of his new ballet *Orpheus* were too complicated for a single player. We kept talking this tutti frutti language, going from English to German to French—"*C'est the end, nicht wahr?*" He told me *the* most amusing definition of sex in the abridged *Larousse*. Some of his anti-Semitic remarks were a little hard to take. Oh no, it wasn't anything extreme, but he kept saying, "Why do they call themselves Russians?"—that sort of thing. I find much more anti-Semitism among educated Americans than among Europeans of a corresponding class. Of course, one is thrown into contact with Jews much more in America than one is in England. I don't believe I'd met a single Jew before going to college.

No, the Devil won't be Envy. He'll be "*le diable de frivolité*." All Stravinsky wanted us to do was to hold his hand. We had to explain why "thou art" was right. He wanted to change it to "thy art." He only knew "art" as a noun.

November 23, 1947

WHA

I don't think one ought to behave queerly in front of women. I'm always shocked when people tell dirty stories or use obscene language in their presence. It isn't good for them. One may want to discusss the subject seriously with one of them, who may be sympathetic and understanding. That's all right. But even there I'm not so sure it's a good idea. Because, you see, women, even the most intelligent of them, can never quite grasp the idea that there are such things as queers. They always feel that the trouble is that the right woman for you just hasn't come along. But they don't doubt that she will.

I don't really think that women should go around with a social group of queers. All right, the people are more amusing, the conversation wittier, but it does terrible things for the girls' egos because they find themselves in a society where they are really not needed. They feel themselves in an important sense left out, and that isn't a good way to feel. One shouldn't confine oneself to queer society. You should look for the nice people in every group. You can always find them.

December 6, 1947

WHA
I just got back from Cambridge this afternoon. I guess I shan't be able to get to the Episcopal Scholars meeting after all. I'll just have to tell them I've been ill. I had a rather nice time at Harvard. I gave my lecture on *Don Quixote*.

The most awful thing has happened—I have to have eight teeth—front ones mind you—pulled out. It's going to be such a bore trotting to and from the dentist, though he assures me they'll be taken care of very soon, whatever that means. I hope I look like Landor—or Dante.

December 10, 1947

WHA

While I was under the anæsthetic I had a dream—it's the second time I've had it. It's all about Chester and salvation. Now I know I can't be damned. The margin of salvation is ever so slight —it was slighter this time than last—but it's there. It was a revelation that God cheats. He gives that extra little push. No, it wasn't a warning—it was an actual revelation.

Dr. Friedman, who's going to make the teeth, is a rather dull orthodontist. It's such a racket they've got, sending you to two dentists, one to extract—that's not a difficult job, but they charge enough for it—and one to make the new ones. What I really begrudge is the time it takes. I don't go to Dr. Kallman because he talks too much. I'm rather shocked he should enjoy circulating the poetry Chester used to write against him.

I'm always amazed at the American practice of allowing one party to a homosexual act to remain passive—it's so undemocratic. Sex must be mutual. You must go to bed with friends or whores, where money makes up the difference in beauty or desire. That's what makes me think that American queers have a guilt complex—there's no feudal tradition here as there is in Europe. I feel if I ask a member of the lower classes there to go to bed, it's his duty to do so.

Americans don't know how to treat whores. They're shocked at the idea, and then they're likely to behave rudely to them. There used to be a good place here before the war—Matty's. That was when people weren't making so much money. It was three dollars and mutual. Of course, Chester wants to be "the only one"—that's the reason he wants non-queers. I prefer myself to go

[89]

to bed with queers, otherwise it's a bore. With queers, it's mutual. I feel increasingly guilty about going to bed with people who aren't friends. Chester is by no means an easy person to get along with. You either have to leave him alone or be as tough as leather. He's had a bad effect on a great many people.

WHA

You know, in Dahomey, there is a group of witch doctors who seem to be the genuine article. They can really kill
people. Some of the French officials crossed them and died very
shortly thereafter. Now the French take good care not to step on
their toes. I'd like to take a trip to see them—to ask them to do
something for me. Yes (*smiling mysteriously*), there's something I
really want them for.

AJA

To get rid of Stalin?

WHA

No, nothing like that. It's something else. They can
really do the job.

AJA

Oh! (*I realized that he was talking about getting them
to make Chester love him faithfully and exclusively again.*) You
can be quite frightening on occasion.

WHA

Oh, I know I'm crazy on some subjects.

AJA

Do you think it's right to ask their help in such matters?

WHA

Oh yes, quite all right.

No, I don't think *Norma* is hysterical. It is the epitome of classicism because situation dominates character. I suppose for people who aren't terribly emotional themselves, the intensity of the music may produce that impression. I cannot see why people like *La Bohème*. The more I go on, the more I dislike Puccini. After all, the whole point of Bohemianism is that there isn't any serious emotion. And the music is supposed to convey emotion. The subject is much better suited to a more intellectual medium—to literature, for instance. Once the people open their mouths and sing, they stop being Bohemians—they really feel. And the discrepancy in the plot! The fourth act is much better by itself, but earlier Mimi and Rodolfo leave each other quite casually, just the way they do in real Bohemia. But then, in that case, why make such a fuss at the end? Why should Mimi come back, why should Rodolfo care? If Mimi really went away with a rich man for Rodolfo's sake, there ought to have been much more feeling on both sides. No, I think liking *La Bohème* is quite dangerous. I don't approve at all.

The only character I can still identify myself with in opera is King Mark in *Tristan*. I don't approve of Hans Sachs's views on art. Why is it that, in music, the amateur wants to keep hearing the same thing and the expert is the only one who wants to hear something new, whereas in literature it is only the expert who wants to reread, while the general public can't go through a work twice? I've decided that opera represents the wilful display of emotions. And it's so odd how the characters always manage to fall in love with unsuitable people.

WHA

The only way to spend New Year's Eve is either quietly with friends or in a brothel. Otherwise when the evening ends and people pair off, someone is bound to be left in tears. Oh yes, I've written about New Year's, but actually that's partly because I was accustomed to spending it alone—the best plan, I think. It's a bigger thing in Scotland and Germany than in England because it originally evolved as a Protestant rival to the traditional festivities at Christmas, which were abhorred as Popish.

You know, one great difficulty in America is the absence of conventions. I know I am very shocked as a teacher when my pupils won't pay me deference. And Chester thinks that when I expect him to get a cab for us it's because I'm me, when it isn't at all. It's simply what an older person expects from a younger one. What people don't realize is that intimacy has its conventions as well as ordinary social intercourse. There are three cardinal rules— don't take somebody else's boyfriend unless you've been specifically invited to do so, don't take a drink without being asked, and keep a scrupulous accounting in financial matters.

When Americans have good manners, they're even better than Europeans'. Manners in society are like conventions in literature.

Oh, my Negro maid has left me. She still works for Rhoda. She didn't show up after that day she cursed at me. It's a disgrace I have to live like this. It's so hard to get servants and accommodation in this country. I make as much money as my father did when he was my age, and he had a wife and three children to support, and he was able to afford a house and an adequate staff of servants while I have to live in two rooms and keep my bed in a working room, something I dislike extremely. My old place on 57th Street had four or five rooms and was much more satisfactory. Of course, there is a bigger servant problem with a bigger place, but they should be much easier to get than they are. I don't want an estate, I just don't see why I shouldn't be comfortable.

January 31, 1948

WHA

We're getting four thousand dollars for the libretto. I'm getting too old to see *Rheingold* from the balcony.

I may send an article attacking the *Kinsey Report* to the *Atlantic* or *Harpers*. It will be written from the standpoint of a representative of the Homintern, so it will have to be anonymous. The *Kinsey Report* is very bad—too many male whores in proportion to the total number interviewed. And he paid too little attention to anal activities. A useful piece of pornography, though.

I must say that James's *Notebooks* annoy me. One reads a passage like "*causons, causons, mon bon*" —his self-justification as a writer—and one thinks it wonderful, a self-revelation like Pascal's *Memorial*. But the *Notebooks* show he was writing like that all the time. And I find that a very suspect attitude for an artist. Kafka's *Diaries* are bad, too. They're so depressing—that terrible Jewish earnestness. It's all right in the novels, but here. . . . Oh, I don't feel the same way about Tchaikovsky's *Diaries*. They're about the woes of a camp, and I don't take that very seriously.

WHA

You know there are no secrets in America. It's quite different in England, where people think of a secret as a shared relationship between two people. That's why you have to have such fantastically strict security regulations over here. That's why I find it so strange that Chester should always go into detail about what he has done in bed. In England, all right, you know someone may be queer or who is sleeping with whom, but that's as far as it goes. You never know the details. It doesn't make any difference whether the secret is innocent or guilty—to tell violates the relationship. It doesn't make any difference to your understanding of Melville to know whether or not he actually went to bed with men.

Allegorical novels like Peacock's are quite different—he simply takes the public personalities of the men and exaggerates them. In England, sex is a subject between mother and son. Your mother is always drawing you aside and telling you your duties toward your father, your father your duties towards your mother, and the maid your duties towards your parents.

Wire-tapping is unheard of in England. Of course, Scotland Yard does tap wires, but only in grave emergencies. It's desperately anxious that its doing so doesn't get out because there would be a terrible fuss raised if it did. Americans have no conception of privacy—these open rooms. If they object to wire-tapping, they do so as a violation of liberty, not of privacy.

Swinburne's *The Whipping Block* has never been published, but it's supposed to be a really good poem, a long epic about whipping. For once he was writing about something he was really interested in. There's so much thrashing in his work when you come to think of it. The language in *Félise* is really much more straightforward than it usually is in his work. He's rather like Shelley—absolutely ga-ga. Well, Shelley may be ga-ga on a little higher plane.

If Swinburne did just want to go on talking, why at least didn't he talk sensibly? I don't like the views of either Shelley or Milton, but one never thinks of Milton as ga-ga. Swinburne does what Shelley wants to do more successfully than Shelley. He lives entirely in a world of words, whereas some reality is always present in Shelley. I don't think Browning was very good in bed. His wife probably didn't care for him very much. He snored and had fantasies about twelve-year-old girls.

April 6, 1948

I HAD lunch at the Pavia with WHA *and Chester.*

WHA

Chester and I are planning a travel book on England with things like meetings in bars with peasants who speak with a regional accent. And we're doing another libretto too—on Berlioz. New York is a very bad place for young people who haven't formed their habits. And I find this nostalgia, this unwillingness to leave New York—I notice it in Chester too—very alarming. Young people should live in small towns. Americans ought to live in Europe.

The next day they sailed for Europe on the Queen Mary.

Afterword

It is a slightly melancholy pleasure forty years on for me to review my record of the conversation of "a great and talkative man," as Auden says in "At the Grave of Henry James."

I first learned to know and admire his work in high school through the old Random House collection of his early writings. So, when I found in the fall of 1946 that he was going to give a series of lectures at the New School for Social Research, I seized on the opportunity to hear the poet in person.

In addition to the regular Wednesday night lectures, he instituted a seminar on Saturday afternoons for a chosen few, which I also attended.

Our acquaintance ripened on the evening of his lecture on *The Merry Wives of Windsor*. He said it was a boring play that had inspired a masterpiece, Verdi's *Falstaff*, so he had decided to spend the lecture hour playing excerpts from the opera. This led to an incipient revolt of the peasants, and I indulged in a counter-demonstration with intoxicating thoughts of the première of Victor Hugo's *Hernani*. In retrospect, though, I must admit that the classical disc jockey didn't help matters by remaining studiously absorbed in the libretto while failing to vouchsafe any summary of its contents to his audience. (But he promised to talk and talk at his next lecture. And talk he did.) After the lecture? concert? I helped him to carry the *Falstaff* albums (78s) the eight blocks back to his apartment.

When I told him I was going to do my course paper on *The Sea and the Mirror*, he at first thought the idea a little crude and rampant. He liked my memorizing Arcite's prayer to Mars in *The Two Noble Kinsmen* for the seminar. But he was cross when I read a speech from a Jonson Christmas masque instead of memorizing it. My excuse was that I was too busy working on the paper. However, after he'd read it, he leaned over my seat on his way to the lecture platform and said, "You've really seen the figure in my carpet." It made my day.

Subsequently, I worked on the chronologies for his *Viking Portable* anthologies of Greek literature and the English poets. Eventually I succeeded Rhoda Jaffe as his secretary, a position whose duties largely consisted of signing checks for his place on Fire Island and forwarding mail to Ischia. I also typed an early version of *The Dyer's Hand* and the libretto of *The Rake's Progress*.

As his paths took him to Ischia and Kirchstetten, so mine led me to Burroughs, Venice and Tangier, and eventually to Athens. Auden visited me occasionally in Venice, and later Chester Kallman and I established a joint table in Athens during the winter months. From 1967 on, I used to spend a week with them in Kirchstetten each autumn and, in 1970, I accompanied them on a pilgrimage to Jerusalem.

Knowing Auden has been one of the greatest privileges of my life.

A. A.

Notes

Notes

In what follows, I have tried to pin down a few of the scores of allusions floating through Auden and Ansen's talk, but I have let many others go by. For example, general biographical outlines are not usually duplicated from Humphrey Carpenter's *W. H. Auden: A Biography* (rev. ed. 1983). In order to use my space constructively, then, the notes are confined to what seemed to me either arcane or forgettable, whether in Auden's work and life, in the arts generally, or in the history of New York during the forties. Each annotation has been triggered by subjective criteria and, in all probability, everyone's knowledge (except my own) will have been underestimated at one point or another. Still, since they are tucked away at the end of the book, I hope these pages will only be consulted when the reader actually *wants* some data. Whatever I don't know, I have passed over in silence.

When possible, convenient editions are cited. In Auden's case, the three basic volumes—*Collected Poems* (1976), *The English Auden* (1977), and *Plays 1928–1938* (1988), all edited by Edward Mendelson—are abbreviated as *CP*, *EA*, and *Plays* respectively.

My thanks are due to Edward Mendelson, who has been a "baltering torrent" of information. A good deal of the scholarship in these notes is his, and I am deeply grateful to him.

N. J.

— 1 —

I've moved from 57th Street. Auden sublet an apartment at 421 West 57th Street from December, 1945 until July, 1946. He moved into 7 Cornelia Street in September, 1946 and lived there (on and off) until October, 1951.

I'm going to be . . . Professor at Harvard. Auden was not, in fact, appointed. Part of the reason, it is said, was because he joked during a lecture there on *Don Quixote* (see p. 88) that he had never finished reading the book.

The Waves. A drama by one of Auden's prep-school masters; it is mentioned in *Letter to Lord Byron, EA,* p. 192.

— 2 —

The Duchess of Malfi. The adaptation, in collaboration with Brecht (though Brecht withdrew his name from the credits after a disagreement), opened on Broadway in October, 1946 in a production directed by George Rylands. It had a short run.

— 3 —

Empson pointed out. In *Some Versions of Pastoral* (1935), p. 27.

Elisabeth Bergner. Bergner, Lee and Carradine were members of the *Duchess* cast. Dame May Whitty performed Auden's radio monologue *The Dark Valley* on CBS on June 2, 1940.

My mother had just died. Auden's mother died on August 21, 1941. In his book *For The Time Being* (1944), Auden ignored the order of composition and printed *The Sea and the Mirror* before the poem *For The Time Being.*

— 5 —

Ratisbon. Often called Regensburg.

Maritain. Jacques Maritain, the philosopher, was French ambassador to the Holy See from 1945 to 1948.

Brecht's lyrics. From "*Gedanken über die Dauer des Exils*" in *Svendborger Gedichte* (1939).

Berlin. Auden lived in Berlin from October, 1928 until May, 1929.

— 6 —

Bennington. Auden was there in the spring of 1946.

— 8 —

the Betjeman anthology. A selection of poems and prose, *Slick but not Streamlined*, was published in July, 1947 with an introduction by Auden.

Miss Phare's book on Hopkins. In the *Criterion*, April, 1934.

The Robe. A 1944 bestseller by Lloyd C. Douglas. Wilson's essay on it is reprinted in *A Literary Chronicle: 1920-1950* (1956). His Archibald MacLeish parody, "The Omelet of A. MacLeish," is in *Night Thoughts* (1961).

the piece about the Jews in music. Published in 1869, the title is *Das*

Judenthum in der Musik. The piece on the "origins of language," is in *Oper und Drama*, also published in 1869.

— 9 —

Trollope wasn't specific enough. See *Journey to a War* (1939), pp. 47-48.

[I] *had to go to work for a living.* After leaving college, Auden first worked as a schoolteacher. From 1940 until late 1944 he had, in fact, received some minimal and irregular financial support from Caroline Newton, a wealthy Pennsylvanian.

— 10 —

complines. The official date for the extinction of the Western Empire is 476. The complines, as we know them, are said to have been drawn up by Saint Benedict around 540.

— 11 —

before you went to Germany. From May until July, 1945, Auden was in Germany with the US Strategic Bombing Survey, officially to interview civilians about the psychological effects of being bombed.

the FBI came round. Probably in July, 1943.

my Phi Beta Kappa poem. Auden read "Under Which Lyre" (*CP*, pp. 259-263) at Harvard on June 3, 1946. James Bryant Conant, Harvard's President, had been a member of the "Interim Committee" advising Truman in the months before the first atomic bomb was dropped on August 6, 1945.

— 12 —

my citizenship papers. Auden became a citizen of the United States in May, 1946. He was never divorced from his wife, Erika Mann. She died in 1969.

— 13 —

I can see myself doing it. In the poem dated "Christmas Day. 1941" and addressed to Chester Kallman, Auden wrote, "Because, on account of you, I have been, in intention, and almost in act, a murderer." See Dorothy J. Farnan's *Auden in Love* (1984), pp. 65-66.

I recognize myself in him sometimes. See "The Cave of Making" in *CP*, pp. 521-523.

A friend. According to Alan Ansen, the "friend" was Chester Kallman.

Victor. For Victor, see *EA*, pp. 218-222, for Joseph, *CP*, pp. 280-284 and and for Edith Gee, *EA*, pp. 214-216.

— 14 —

the best one I ever did. A reconstructed version of the ballad, "Sue," was published by the Sycamore Press (Oxford) in 1977.

— 15 —

I don't dislike Wordsworth. But see *Letter to Lord Byron* in *EA*, p. 183.

— 16 —

"Chicane in furs." From *The Dunciad* (1743), IV.28.

"Pædicabo." Catullus XVI; *"Odi et amo"* is LXXXV.

duet between Brünnhilde and Waltraute. In *Götterdämmerung*, Act I.

— 17 —

"Das ist kein Mann." In *Siegfried*, Act III.

Tristan or Don Giovanni. See "In Sickness and In Health" in *CP*, pp. 247-249.

— 18 —

Italian Symphony. By Mendelssohn.

Kaputt. Published in America in 1946.

— 19 —

Randall Jarrell. See his essay "Freud to Paul: The Stages of Auden's Ideology" (1945), reprinted in *The Third Book of Criticism* (1969), p. 154.

"O Tell Me. . . ." The poem beginning "Some say that Love's a little boy," in *EA*, pp. 230-231. Auden met Chester Kallman on April 6, 1939, two and a half months after his arrival in America.

a poem I did in the early thirties. See "Easily, my dear, you move, easily your head" in *EA*, pp. 152-154.

I'm really a sanguine person. See "Precious Five" in *CP*, pp. 447-450.

in Transylvania. Auden visited Transylvania in August, 1934 during a motoring holiday, his "Dracula trip." See "Since" in *CP*, pp. 584-585, for a memory of it. For Hammerfest, see his poem of that name in *CP*, pp. 545-546.

— 20 —

have left high school teaching. By this time, Auden was making his living as a freelance lecturer and critic.

resident poets at Michigan. Auden taught at Ann Arbor from October, 1941 to May, 1942. Bridges spent three months there in 1924 when he was eighty years old.

Eliot is perfectly devastating. Eliot's comments are in "The Music of Poetry" (1942), reprinted in *On Poetry and Poets* (1957).

the Professorship of Poetry. Arnold was the Professor from 1857 to 1867, Ker from 1920 to 1923, and Ernest de Selincourt, the Wordsworth scholar, from 1928 to 1933. Auden himself was Professor from 1956 to 1960. Eliot was never appointed to the Professorship, but he won the Nobel Prize in 1948. Pearl Buck won it in 1938, and Sinclair Lewis in 1930.

— 21 —

Bennett Cerf. One of the founders of Random House and Auden's first American editor.

a house in Sea Cliff. Auden lent Chester Kallman's father the money to buy a house in Sea Cliff, Long Island. See *Auden in Love,* pp. 125-127.

"Ozean! Du Ungeheuer!" From Weber's *Oberon.*

contract for The Age. Auden wanted the book to resemble a treatise on mining techniques which he had read as a child.

— 22 —

and into the OED. Auden is repeatedly cited in the *OED Supplement.* See note to p. 67.

a very early play. The Enemies of a Bishop (1929), see *Plays.*

— 23 —

Around Lydgate's time. Lydgate's dates are c. 1370-1449. Chaucer issues his warning in *Troilus and Criseyde* (c. 1385) V.1793-1799.

posts like the one they gave MacLeish. Archibald MacLeish held various posts in the Roosevelt Administration. From 1944-1945 he was Assistant Secretary of State.

Margaret [Truman]. The President's daughter. See p. 35.

— 24 —

Cæli, Lesbia nostra. Catullus LVIII.

Nicolson. Harold Nicolson met Proust in March, 1919. Nicolson's wife was Vita Sackville-West.

que le sable était beau! In *Si le Grain Ne Meurt* (1926) Part 2, Chapter 1.

an exciting old Welsh epic. Aneirin's *Y Gododdin.*

— 25 —

a superior type of riddle. See "T the Great" in *CP*, pp. 457-458.

Thésée. The 1946 novella by Gide.

worshipping Voltaire. See *Mon Coeur Mis à Nu*, section XVIII.

— 26 —

Athalia. The oratorio by Handel.

I cut out the Housman poem. "A. E. Housman" was not reprinted in *Collected Poetry* (1945), the first intensive sifting of his work that Auden made. It is in *EA*, p. 238. Auden refers to the Housman poem beginning "Ho, everyone that thirsteth" in *More Poems* (not *Further Poems*), published in 1936. Forster's review appeared in the *Listener* on November 11, 1936.

I agree with Nietzsche. His criticisms are in *Der Fall Wagner*, section 6.

— 27 —

[the Pope's] broadcast in English. Pius XII broadcast an appeal for funds to Catholic schoolchildren on February, 19, 1947.

Spellman. Francis Spellman had been the Cardinal-Archbishop of New York since 1939.

In Copenhagen. Auden and Christopher Isherwood were in Copenhagen for a few days in January, 1935 working on *The Dog Beneath the Skin.*

[George V's] willingness to go along. In 1910, at the beginning of his reign, George V cooperated with Asquith's attempts to pass the controversial "People's Budget" and to dilute the power of the Tory peers.

Shaw was just being amusing. See *The Apple Cart* (1928).

— 28 —

the King's Poetry Medal. George V died on January 20, 1936. Auden received the King's Gold Medal for Poetry from George VI on November 23, 1937.

— 29 —

my friend who works at the broadcasting station. Nicolas Nabokov, who became the first head of the Russian broadcast unit of the Voice of America in 1947.

Mirsky. Prince D. S. Mirsky, the historian of Russian literature, was arrested in 1937 and died in prison in 1939.

Romanitas. For Auden's concept of "*Romanitas*," see his introduction to James's *The American Scene* (1946), partially reprinted in *The Dyer's Hand* (1961), pp. 318-321.

l'esprit de Voltaire. I have been unable to locate this phrase, but see *Mon Coeur Mis à Nu* for blasts against Voltaire. See also *New Year Letter* in CP, p. 164.

— 30 —

Colonel McCormick. Robert R. McCormick, publisher, editor and leader-writer of the *Chicago Tribune*, was well-known for his anti-Communist positions.

his last days underground in Berlin. Hugh Trevor-Roper's *The Last Days of Hitler* was published in February, 1947.

in Paris before the war. Auden was in Paris in early December, 1938.

— 31 —

[Laval's] trial. Laval's short trial in October, 1945 was turned—by both prosecution and defense—into a symbolic political event.

— 33 —

Smuts. General Smuts, the South African Prime Minister, called in March, 1947 for a United Africa in order to promote international peace.

"It's all straw." See William of Tocco's *Vita Sancti Thomæ Aquinatis* (1318), and Kierkegaard's *Journals* (1938) ed. A. Dru, p. 134.

— 35 —

Margaret Truman. The President's daughter made her debut as a professional singer in Detroit on March 16, 1947. Fifteen million people, at that time the largest audience ever for a performing artist, listened to her live broadcast. The aria was actually from *La Perle du Brésil* by Félicien David. Florence Foster Jenkins, the President of the National Society of Patriotic Women, died in 1944.

Lawrence. Auden was reviewing *The Portable D. H. Lawrence.* His essay appeared in the *Nation* on April 26, 1947.

— 36 —

the Memorial. A record of the visionary experience Pascal had during the night of November 23, 1654. See "Pascal" in *EA*, pp. 451-453.

— 38 —

algebraic symbols. See the lines of *New Year Letter* (1940) beginning "Art in intention is mimesis" in *CP*, p. 162.

— 39 —

Ken Lewars. His thesis, "The Quest in Auden's Poems and Plays" (1947), was by no means the first to be written on Auden.

the one good thing Galsworthy did. His *Old English* (1924).

— 40 —

My brother-in-law Borgese. Guiseppe Antonio Borgese married Auden's sister-in-law Elizabeth Mann in November, 1939. The epithalamion that Auden wrote for them is in *EA*, pp. 453-456.

words like se tartuffiser. French dictionaries record only the verb *tartufier* used by, amongst others, Madame de Sévigné.

Swarthmore. Auden taught there from September, 1942 to April, 1945.

— 41 —

Fire Island. Auden was part owner of a cabin at Cherry Grove on Fire Island. See "Pleasure Island" in *CP*, pp. 265-267.

[Lawrence's] *girlfriends.* Auden and Chester Kallman met Frieda Lawrence and some of Lawrence's followers during their trip to New Mexico in 1939.

— 42 —

I don't approve of Pound's politics. However, in 1946, Auden threatened to withdraw his work from Random House when they proposed cutting Pound out of an anthology. In 1949 he was one of the judges who awarded the first Bollingen Prize to Pound.

— 43 —

Ker. The book is *Collected Essays of W. P. Ker* (1925) ed. C. Whibley.

— 44 —

Eliot's The Sacred Wood. Published in 1920.

Empson's two books. By this time, Empson had published *Seven Types of Ambiguity* (1930) and *Some Versions of Pastoral* (1935).

The Case of Wagner. Auden read the book shortly after he came to the United States in 1939 (see note to p. 26).

— 45 —

the Grammar. Kenneth Burke's *A Grammar of Motives* (1945). Auden shared a cottage with Burke at Bennington in 1946.

the Carmen Sæculare. Probably the cycle called *Bucolics* in *CP*, pp. 426-435. The plans for *Underground Life* never came to anything, although Auden apparently considered the project throughout the summer of 1947.

— 46 —

detective novels. Auden was preoccupied with detective stories at this time. His essay on them, "The Guilty Vicarage," appeared in *Harper's Magazine* in May, 1948. It is reprinted in *The Dyer's Hand* (1961). H. M. (Sir Henry Merrivale) and Dr. Fell are detectives created by John Dickson Carr. Faith Baldwin was a prolific popular novelist.

Dewey was bidding for the Homintern vote. Governor Dewey of New York vetoed the "Desmond Bill" on April 11, 1947.

that spy place. In Brooklyn, a national scandal. Senator David Walsh, Democrat of Massachusetts, died in June, 1947. Sumner Welles was a diplomat, author and pundit.

— 47 —

excluded from the draft. Auden was turned down by the Army in September, 1942.

Klaus Mann. Klaus Mann was a correspondent for *Stars and Stripes*, a services' newspaper, from 1942 until 1945.

OSS. The Office of Strategic Services was an intelligence agency. AMG was the Allied Military Government (of the Occupied Territories).

— 48 —

Inspector French. A Freeman Wills Crofts detective.

— 49 —

O'Duffy ended up. He died in 1944.

say something like "rod." See "The Chambermaid's Second Song" in *Last Poems and Plays* (1940). In the summer of 1948, Auden wrote his pornographic poem, "The Platonic Blow."

— 51 —

as late as your time. Ansen graduated from Harvard in 1942. Auden was at Oxford from 1925 to 1928. For his views on austerity then, see the stanza beginning "All youth's intolerant certainty was mine as" in *Letter to Lord Byron, EA*, p. 195.

a great deal of humorous poetry. "King Bolo and his Great Black Kween," partially reprinted in *The Letters of T. S. Eliot* (1988), Vol. 1. Eliot drafted his play *The Cocktail Party* in 1948.

On a Note of Triumph. Corwin's radio drama hailing the victory in Europe was broadcast on CBS on May 8, 1945 and published in book form the same year.

The Chase. This is the title that Auden himself chose for an earlier (1934) version of *The Dog Beneath the Skin* (1935). *The Fronny* (1930) was a different and now lost play. The friend he refers to was Francis Turville-Petre, whom he and Isherwood met in Berlin in 1929. The "chunks" of *The Changing Face of England* (1926) are mainly in the choruses of the play. For details, see *Plays.*

"Speech from a Play." Published in *New Verse*, February, 1935. It is from *The Chase*. Parts of it draw on the "long poem" called "In the Year of My Youth" (1932-1933), ed. Lucy S. MacDiarmid in the *Review of English Studies*, August, 1978, pp. 281-309. "The Malverns" is in *EA*, pp. 141-144.

— 52 —

"Wafna." See *The Age of Anxiety* in CP, p. 368.

— 53 —

an early essay on Dante. In *The Use of Poetry and the Use of Criticism* (1933), p. 95. The Milton essay which he alludes to, "Milton I" (1936), is reprinted in *On Poetry and Poets* (1957).

Shakespeare's philosophy is stoicism. See Eliot's essay "Shakespeare and the Stoicism of Seneca" (1927) in *Selected Essays 1917-1932* (1932). Edgar's line is in *King Lear*, V.2. The drift of Eliot's essay is not really what Auden suggests here.

a lecture on Milton. "Milton II," the lecture in which Eliot revised his view of Milton, was given at the Frick Museum. It is reprinted in *On Poetry and Poets* (1957). *Notes Towards the Definition of Culture* was published in November, 1948 (and reviewed by Auden in the *New Yorker* on April 23, 1949).

– 54 –

topophiliac poet. Auden used the term in his *Slick but not Streamlined* introduction to describe Betjeman's poetry. For the *Argo* see *Paradiso* 33.96 and for Lucca, see *Inferno* 33.30. Auden may already have been working on his review of *The Portable Dante* which was published in the *New York Times* on June 29, 1947.

Harold Ross. The editor of the *New Yorker*. Auden's poem appeared there on January 6, 1940.

– 55 –

Orville Prescott. The daily book critic for the *New York Times*.

I can't go without a job completely. Auden had no regular job during the winter of 1947-1948, although he seems to have applied in December for a post with the Cultural Relations division of the Occupying Forces in Germany. His major literary project during this period was *The Rake's Progress*.

a book on primitive American poetry. Auden does not appear to have written an introduction to this anthology. Suzanne Degnan was a child who was kidnapped and murdered in Chicago in 1946.

– 56 –

the scene for wild parties. That summer, Auden went to a party at the Fire Island Hotel dressed as Cardinal Pirelli.

– 57 –

Grand Canyon. Forster rode a mule down into the Grand Canyon on May 15, 1947.

this teacher rating business. In March, 1947 the State legislature voted to adopt a merit-rating system for public school teachers. The decision was still controversial in May.

— 58 —

"Our revels." From *The Tempest*, IV.1.

— 59 —

the Tennyson anthology. Auden's selection from Tennyson's poems was published in England in December, 1946.

that dialogue. Act II, the Fairy Queen to Private Willis.

— 60 —

An Oxford Tragedy. A 1933 detective story by J. C. Masterman.

— 61 —

Ted Spencer. Theodore Spencer was a professor of English literature at Harvard. Auden used him as a "literary confessor" during the 1940s. He died in 1949.

"in hideous ruin." From *Paradise Lost* I.46-47.

— 62 —

"concatenation." See *The Age of Anxiety*, CP, p. 353.

Gorbuduc. The 1561 drama by Norton and Sackville.

The Importance of Being Earnest. A production opened in New York in March, 1947.

— 63 —

Grock. A Swiss clown.

L'il Abner. The strip drawn by Al Capp. Terry in *Terry and the Pirates* was a major in the US Air Force. *Gasoline Alley's* hero, Skeezix Wallet, was the first character in an American comic strip to grow and age. All these strips were syndicated in the New York *Daily News*.

Bradford. E. E. Bradford (1860-1944), the author of thirteen books of poetry, was vicar of Holy Trinity, Nordelph, Norfolk. S. E. Cottam (1863-1945?) was vicar of Wootton, Berks.

— 65 —

Mary McCarthy. Mary McCarthy was divorced from Edmund Wilson in 1946. In the same year she married Bowden Broadwater and Wilson married Elena Mumm Thornton.

— 66 —

never had to live with [a maiden aunt]. Alan Ansen was living with his maiden aunt in Woodmere, Long Island, during this period.

the Whatmoughs. Joshua Whatmough was the chairman of Harvard's Department of Comparative Philology.

— 67 —

include in Les Poètes Maudits. Rimbaud, Mallarmé and Corbière.

a guidebook to England. Neither the guidebook nor the Firbank anthology was ever published.

the word "Homintern." In spite of Auden's efforts to legitimize this and several other words of gay slang by using them in his prose, "Homintern" has not yet surfaced in any major English language dictionary.

— 68 —

detective stories. Auden twice reviewed detective stories for the *Daily Telegraph* during the winter of 1936-1937.

to ease the blow. J. Donald Adams lost his job as editor of the *New York Times Book Review* in 1943.

— 69 —

come back to town. Auden had returned from a summer on Fire Island the previous day.

the article for Harper's. Auden's article, "The Mythical Sex," appeared in *Harper's Bazaar* in October, 1947. "I Like It Cold" appeared in *House and Garden* in December, 1947.

— 70 —

"Law Like Love." For these poems, see *EA*, Part VI. "The Capital" contains the lines "hinting at the forbidden like a wicked uncle, / Night after night to the farmer's children you beckon."

Birmingham. Auden's family home was in Birmingham.

Rosetta's Song. For this and the other passages from *The Age of Anxiety* referred to here, see *CP*, pp. 361, 408, 380, 406, 408 (again), 357.

— 71 —

Michael Innes. The pseudonym used by the Oxford don J. I. M. Stewart for his detective stories.

— 72 —

a talk on Yeats. "Yeats as an Example," the lecture which Auden gave in December, 1947, was printed in the *Kenyon Review* in the spring of 1948. The poem he mentions here is "Byzantium" in *The Winding Stair and Other Poems* (1933).

his people weren't related to the Butlers. See Yeats's poem "Pardon, Old Fathers" in *Responsibilities* (1914). Butler is the family name of the Earls of Ormonde.

a selected edition of Pope. This was never published. "Bare the mean Heart. . . ." is from "The First Satire of the Second Book of Horace Imitated," line 108. Johnson's remark is in his *Life of Pope.* "And beastly Skelton. . . ." is from "The First Epistle of the Second Book of Horace, Imitated," line 38.

— 73 —

Toye's book. The musicologist Francis Toye's book on Rossini is called *Rossini: a Study in Tragi-comedy* (1934) and the one on Verdi, *Giusseppe Verdi: His Life and Works* (1931).

Werther. A production by the City Center Opera Company of Massenet's *Werther* opened in October, 1947.

— 74 —

an anthology of Greek literature. Edited and introduced by Auden, *The Portable Greek Reader* was published in September, 1948 in a somewhat slimmer version than the one outlined here. There was no Christian section. The introduction was reprinted as "The Greeks and Us" in *Forewords and Afterwords* (1973).

— 75 —

Landor's epigrams. Both Oxford and Cambridge University Presses published selections from Landor in 1946.

the Ben Shahn exhibition. A major retrospective at the Museum of Modern Art opened in October, 1947.

— 76 —

an opera with Stravinsky. *The Rake's Progress* eventually opened in Venice in August, 1951. Auden stayed with the Stravinskys in Los Angeles from November 11 to November 18, 1947 (see p. 86). Kallman and Auden finished the libretto in February, 1948. Stravinsky's Mass for mixed chorus and double wind quintet was first performed in 1948. Auden perhaps reassures Ansen that there will be no friction in the light of Stravinsky's famous quarrel with Gide during work on *Perséphone* (1933-1934).

— 77 —

separate publication. The libretto was published in August, 1951.

— 79 —

Denny Foutts. Fouts, an American, divided his life between Europe and the United States. In the early forties, he became friendly with Christopher Isherwood and provided the basis for "Paul" in *Down There on a Visit* (1962). He also appears in Truman Capote's *Answered Prayers* (1987). Fouts became dependent on alcohol and heroin and died, apparently of a heart attack, in Rome in 1949. Lord Tredegar, neither the first nor the last of his titled lovers, died in 1954.

Inverchapel. Baron Inverchapel, the British ambassador to Washington from May, 1946 to March, 1948. Auden and Isherwood first met him in Shanghai, where he was then ambassador, in 1938. The *Chicago Tribune* supported American isolationism.

— 80 —

the ONI. Office of Naval Intelligence.

— 83 —

[Brecht's] *party card*. On October 30, 1947 Brecht denied before the Committee that he had ever been a member of the Communist party.

— 84 —

proportional representation. The New York City electorate was about to vote on a proposal to repeal the proportional representation method of choosing City Council members.

— 85 —

Titus Groan. The first volume of the Gormenghast trilogy (1946-1959) by Mervyn Peake.

Thingummy. The writer was, in fact, Geoffrey Gorer whose piece, "The American Character," appeared in *Life* on August 18, 1947.

— 86 —

I'm just back from California. See note to p. 76.

— 88 —

my lecture on Don Quixote. "The Ironic Hero" was given at Harvard on December 4, 1947 and published in *Third Hour, IV* (1949). See note to p. 13.

— 89 —

I don't go to Dr. Kallman. Chester Kallman's father was a dentist.

— 93 —

I've written about New Year's. For instances, see "A Happy New Year" in *EA*, pp. 444-451 and *New Year Letter, CP,* pp. 161-193.

Rhoda. Auden's affair with Rhoda Jaffe seems to have been over by now, but they remained friends.

— 94 —

My old place on 57th Street. See note to p. 1.

— 95 —

Rheingold. A new production was to open at the Metropolitan Opera in February, 1948.

the Kinsey Report. Published in early January, 1948. No such piece by Auden is known.

Causons, mon bon. See *The Notebooks of Henry James*, p. 348. This passage is from some notes made by James in 1909-1910 for a novel, *The Ivory Tower*, that he later abandoned. They were printed as "The 'K. B.' Case and 'Mrs. Max,'" in the edition of the *Notebooks* published in the autumn of 1947. However, since Auden had already used phrases from the passage in his poem "At the Grave of Henry James" (1941)—it is in *Selected Poems* (1979), pp. 119-123—it seems likely that he knew the invocation from *The Letters of Henry James*

(1920), where the editor, Percy Lubbock, quotes it in pp. xx-xxi. Tchaikovsky's *Diaries* were reviewed by Auden in the *New York Times* on December 2, 1945.

— 96 —

Swinburne's The Whipping Block. For *The Flogging Block* (1861-1881) see *Swinburne, A Literary Biography* (1932) by Georges Lafourcade. "Félise" is in *Poems and Ballads* (1866).

— 98 —

We're doing another libretto. Called *On the Way*, it was to have dealt with the relations of Berlioz, Mendelssohn and Rossini to the Muse. Auden and Kallman sketched an outline and tried to interest Stravinsky, but nothing was ever finished.

they sailed for Europe. This was Auden's first visit since the war. He returned to New York in mid-September, 1948.